Endorsements

Here is a book that will both touch your heart and lift your soul to new heights. It is a book about hope in crisis and light in the midst of dark night. Read it, reread it, share it. It is that kind of book. __Linus Mundy, creator of CareNotes and author of numerous articles and books in the religious press, including SIMPLY MERTON, a book summarizing the work and beliefs of the famous Trappist monk, Thomas Merton.

In *Soul Provider* we witness a pilgrimage from suffering and death to new life. As Shirley companioned her young daughter in her struggles with cancer, each came to know "the tender mercy of God," especially through the compassionate love shown by friends and the medical staff. Since the untimely death of her daughter, Shirley continues to deepen her relationship with God through contemplative prayer. In her service to others she shows by word and deed "the tender mercy of God," especially to women who are incarcerated. As a Benedictine Oblate Shirley embodies the Benedictine motto "Ora et Labora" – Pray and Work. *Soul Provider* is a good read for all who seek meaning in suffering and death.

Sister Kathy Huber, OSB, Sisters of St. Benedict, Ferdinand, Indiana

"There are books that sometimes come along which have forced me to look at life in a whole new way. *Soul Provider* is one of those books. It is the true story of how a family healed from an unimaginable tragedy through the help of family, friends, community and faith. You will be inspired by this book, and it might heal your own soul."

Brenda Robertson Stewart, author of *POWER IN THE BLOOD* and numerous mystery novels, editor, artist

What Shirley France shares in this powerful story is more than just feel-good and inspiring: it's the stuff of life-changing and impactful conversion. Allow the Holy Spirit to move and work through these words and stand back: you're sure to be changed and moved!

- Sarah Reinhard, author and blogger, SnoringScholar.com

Soul Provider

Soul Provider

THE STORY OF GOD'S
ABIDING PRESENCE

Shirley France

ISBN-13: 9781974674145
ISBN-10: 1974674142

In gratitude to Trista

Acknowledgements

§

FEW ENDEAVORS IN LIFE ARE completed alone. I would like to express my deepest gratitude to the people who helped and encouraged me to bring this book to publication.

To those who lived the journey with our family, I am thankful: Christ the King Parish of Madisonville, Kentucky as well as our sisters and brothers in Christ from the entire Madisonville community. Without their prayers, acts of kindness and generosity, we could not have survived. I've often reflected about how God, in His wisdom and love, placed us in the care of His people at this specific place at this specific time.

Believing that when the pupil is ready the teacher appears, Father Delma Clemons, our Madisonville parish priest, was our spiritual guide on this entire journey. Without whose love and companionship all of us would have been lost, we thank God for his constant care, witness, courage, love and humor. Father Delma continues to teach and inspire us to stay on the journey while also sharing the journey with others.

I express my deep gratitude to those who contributed by editing throughout various stages of manuscript development. Among those are Linus Mundy, Tom and Barbara Clinton, and Brenda Stewart. Brenda Stewart has been my mentor throughout the writing process and has offered words of encouragement that kept me going through the last five years of writing, editing and publishing considerations.

Several friends read the manuscript and provided helpful feedback and encouragement. Among them were Judy Donley, our friend and fellow parishioner at Madisonville, Tara Steckler, Trista's godmother and dear friend, Deacon Charles Knight from Our Lady of Lourdes parish and Sally Halas, my sister in Christ from Indiana. Their support and perspectives were invaluable to me. Several readers who also graciously contributed their time by reading the manuscript include Father Pat Toner, my confessor and friend plus Ken Montera, my friend and former Executive V. P. at Bath & Body Works Corporation. The gift of time these people gave me by reading about our story is a genuine act of love and I'm grateful for each contribution of feedback.

I'm especially grateful to my dear friend of nearly twenty years, Sandy Tucker, who has been a beacon of spiritual support through prayer, and to my husband, Steph, for never giving up on the idea that the words from my journals would one day become this book.

And finally last, but not least, I thank our dear son, Stephan, who continues to reprise humorous stories about when we were the four us before we became the three of us. These words sit in a sacred and intimate space our family holds in our hearts forever.

CHAPTER 1

§

OUT THE FRONT DOOR I went, as if I knew where I was going. But I certainly didn't. After walking for who knows how long, I noticed a little bar, a venue totally out of character for me to frequent. But then again, everything about our lives was totally out of the norm. *What the heck is norm?* I wondered. I walked into the door of the bar like I'd been there many times and took a seat on a stool at the long counter facing my vast assortment of liquor options. Service being exceptional, the female bartender promptly asked what I needed. *Great question*, I thought. I explained that I had no money, my child was in recovery from brain cancer and I desperately needed a change of scenery to think. Smiling back at me as though she hadn't heard the part about me not having any money, she asked again, "What can I get you?"

CHAPTER 2

§

IT ALL BEGAN IN 1970 when Stephan France and I were married. We lived in a small, one- hundred-year-old, two-story home near Akron University. Purchased for $10,000 with $100 down on a 30-year loan, that $80-a-month house payment included taxes and insurance. "What a deal!" my husband would often say.

Idealistic, in love, young and very poor, we discovered a little before we got married, we were expecting our first child. That did not stop us from having a beautiful traditional Catholic wedding at St. Vincent's Catholic Church in Akron—as had the last two generations of the France family before us. In fact, we were definitely a couple with a customized agenda for our life together without much concern about what other people thought. This attitude was a little tough on my parents but they loved us unconditionally and were a great support, even though Stephan was rather "hippie-looking" as the lead singer in a rock band and I was a part-time hairdresser while carrying our child. We were incredibly happy together and quite proud of our home, our love for each other and the life we were building. It made sense to us. It was perfect for us. We didn't need much in the way of material things. It was a good life.

Because we were very poor and I mean *very*, we often drove to my parents' home in Portage Lakes where we could always count on a great meal and a competitive game of cards taking us long into the evening. All my brothers, their wives and my sister loved hanging out at Mom and Dad's house because my parents had time for us. As retirees, they loved it when family showed up at any time and often asked us to spend the night because Dad loved waking up to us all having breakfast together in the morning. Our parents appreciated and supported us, which was a precious gift.

It was nearing time for our baby to be born when Stephan realized he had signed a contract for his band to play a gig out of town. This made me a little nervous because I most certainly wanted my husband present for the birth of our first child! As it turned out, Trista Mae France, 7 pounds and 6 ounces, was born one day before Stephan had to leave. "Look at all that dark hair," everyone commented when they saw little Trista for the very first time. In fact, her baby pictures looked very much like her dad's and mine. She was beautiful, perfect.

Because I am a hairdresser, I do know that most of the time a newborn baby's hair will fall out and then new hair will grow. Trista's never did fall out. In fact, at five months old, I was able to make two good-sized ponytails. As a hairdresser, I was totally filled with pride about this.

Having Trista solidified our family into a "real" family. We enjoyed her so much that 16 months later we had another child, Stephan Edward France II, who was born two weeks early. Thank God for that because he weighed 8 pounds and 6 ounces in a premature birth.

With two children in diapers at the same time, it was challenging. Disposable diapers didn't come into being until Stephan was born and he was highly allergic to them. With no washing machine and no money to go to a laundromat, I washed diapers in our only bathtub and hung them up to dry in the basement. I really did not mind. I loved being a wife, a mom and doing all the domestic chores. I really did!

Dad did eventually take pity on me though and gifted us with a new washer and dryer not long after Stephan was born.

Steph, my husband, was still living the "rock star" dream and traveled with the band while I stayed home taking care of our little ones. I remember being afraid at night sometimes right after I put the children to bed. To calm my wild imagination, I got out my Bible, crawled into our bed and read until I fell asleep. It worked for me every time. I especially enjoyed the Old Testament stories that I found as interesting as any fiction I had ever read.

It didn't take all that long for Steph to realize that living his "rock star" dream wasn't providing sufficient income to support our family. So he got a job at City Hospital for a short time, then one at Goodyear Tire and Rubber Company building tires, a job his father also did at B.F. Goodrich. How perfect! We now had benefits, a steady income, a dependable work schedule and options for overtime. God certainly answered my prayers about this. But it didn't last long. Only nine months into his new position, Steph was informed that the Akron Goodyear plant was going to close but that they were giving him options for moving our family to another plant in another city if he chose to stay with Goodyear. Very excited about this opportunity and ready for a new adventure, we moved to Madisonville, Kentucky, as did my sister who was now married to Steph's brother Greg who also worked for Goodyear. Fifty families from Akron migrated south to start new lives in Kentucky at about the same time.

With me, Trista and young Stephan in our Volkswagen, Steph in a U-Haul truck packed with everything we owned, it took 13 hours to reach our Kentucky destination. While on the long drive I reflected that our children at three and four years old would never remember living in Akron and that Madisonville would be their home where they would grow up, go to school, become adults. It made me a little sad to consider this and leaving my parents, but at the same time I was excited to begin this new life with my family. Besides, without the U-Haul, a nine-hour drive to and from Akron was doable in a day. Piece of cake, I decided.

Life was good in Kentucky. Stephan and Trista were doing well in school, Steph's job at Goodyear went well enough for us to have a new brick ranch home built and I was working again as a hairdresser.

My sister, Pam, and her family built a similar style home one lot away from ours on the same street. The only challenge was that all of us missed our parents terribly. So that first couple of years living down south we really heated up the highway north to Akron and my parents did the same heading south to see us, too.

Probably because Trista looked a lot like me when she was young, my Dad grew very attached to her and they shared a special relationship. As "buddies", they began writing each other letters. Forever the teacher, I'm certain this was a partial ploy to enhance Trista's writing and reading skills. Dad never missed even a covert opportunity to help anyone learn something new. I loved that about him.

Sometimes Trista would go to Akron to stay with Mom and Dad for several weeks during the summer when school was out. On these occasions she would write to us in Kentucky to tell us everything she was doing with her Grandma and "Puppa," as she called my dad. The content of one of those letters really stands out to me. "Dear Mom and Dad and Stephan, Puppa and Grandma know exactly what they are going to do today and what time they plan to do it. They have a list written down for every day. When we are done with a job, Puppa lets me cross that job off the list. Why can't we do that at our house so we will know what to do? Love, Trista"

CHAPTER 3

§

ALL WAS GOING WELL FOR us in Kentucky. It was going so well that we second-mortgaged our home to build my dream salon which became a vehicle for us to get more involved in the community as we made many new friends. One new acquaintance was Fr. Glahn, the priest from Christ the King Catholic Church just up the road not far from our house. We met at a party through mutual friends and we instantly liked him because he was funny, authentic and was accepting of every-one he was around. At this time we were attending the Cumberland Presbyterian Church where I was the choir director. But Fr. Glahn, in a way, pursued us as friends by often stopping in at our house for dinner unannounced or staying over after dinner to watch the new show on television called *Saturday Night Live* which showcased con-troversial topics that totally pushed the envelope of socially accept-able humor. We liked Fr. Glahn and he became a genuine friend.

After months of pop-in visits, I realized that there was prob-ably more on Fr. Glahn's agenda than my less-than-gourmet home-cooked meals. One evening after a meal while chatting, Fr. Glahn asked me why I hadn't learned more about the Catholic Church since Steph was raised Catholic and we were married in the Catholic Church, although I had chosen at that time not to convert. I explained that I just couldn't believe that weird Catholic stuff like worshiping Mary, the statues and going to a priest for confession. The whole Catholic thing was really out there for me after having been raised Presbyterian with my Mom as the Director of Christian Education at our huge church for many years. I was totally rooted in my faith and denomination.

Interestingly though, I remembered Tara Steckler, my friend and stylist from our salon, saying to me that she believed I'd be Catholic one day. When she said that, I laughed, pooh-poohed that notion big-time and hadn't given this idea another thought until now.

Fr. Glahn challenged me to simply participate in the R.C.I.A. classes to learn about the Catholic faith and then ask the Holy Spirit to guide my decision to become a Catholic or not. He informed me that classes were on Thursday evenings. Well, praise God! That let me off the hook because Thursday was the late-work night at our salon. To miss work on that night was out of the question. I guessed that was settled.

Early the following Monday morning Fr. Glahn called to inform me that the new priest who would be taking over as pastor of Christ the King church once he moved on, would be willing to give me and a sponsor private instruction on Monday mornings, the day the salon was closed. I had no more excuses and Tara Steckler agreed to be my sponsor.

Wondering how this decision to attend classes about the Catholic faith would sit with my Mom who had never had a Catholic in her family, I wrote her a letter explaining the series of events that led to this decision. I remember that I had just settled onto a seat on a plane headed somewhere to teach a hairdressing class as I had often done on weekends, when I opened the letter from my Mom responding to my intentions to learn about the Catholic Church.

Mom had been raised a Baptist, but then worshiped her adult life as a Presbyterian, so it was not a total surprise that she would respond in her usual loving way. "If you want to worship Mary, that's your business, honey, and don't let anyone tell you differently. I love you and know that God will work all this out," she wrote. It made me chuckle when I read the words but then I reflected on the unconditional love my Mom had for all five of her kids. It was a loving thing to say and I was grateful for her words.

R.C.I.A. classes began in August of that year and by four sessions with the new Catholic priest, Fr. Delma, and Tara my sponsor, I knew I was called to worship as a Catholic. In fact, in September our family plus my mom and dad, went on a trip to London so I could attend advanced haircutting and color classes at a world-famous cosmetology school. While in England, Steph bought a little nine-karat gold crucifix necklace for me and I cherished it. I would rub my hands over the crucifix many times a day as a reminder of Christ's suffering, dying and rising for me. In my heart, I was already Catholic.

While on this trip to England, we visited cathedrals and learned about English historical figures whose lives were impacted by their faith. This topic was riveting for me. I couldn't get enough. As I learned and talked about the Catholic faith, our children learned simultaneously. Interestingly, my husband Steph was learning, too. Born into a Catholic family and attending private Catholic schools through 12th grade did not make him an expert on Catholicism. However, he did have unique insights about what we were learning and it was refreshing that all four of us were learning together and it seemed so right for us. Mom and Dad, both former schoolteachers, were also highly engaged to learn about the historical implications leading to the birth of the Protestant Church from out of the Catholic Church. What an amazing trip that I intended to be all about new technical hair techniques which turned out to be a faith journey for all six of us.

With new perspective about my method of worship and the continuation of the R.C.I.A. classes, the only hurdle to becoming Catholic remaining for me was confession. Just the idea of revealing to Fr. Delma, the new priest, everything I could remember I had ever done wrong or failed to do, was terrifying to me and I told him so. Since Fr. Delma's former position prior to coming to Madisonville was as chaplain at Eddyville Prison for 13 years, I was somewhat assured that I had nothing to share that he probably hadn't already heard from someone else's confession. Obviously, I was missing the point of confession somewhere in all this by comparing my sins to those of poor incarcerated souls, but Fr. Delma was kind and tolerant of my learning about this for the first time. He assured me that my confession was to Jesus, not to him personally and that it would be liberating to begin this new faith journey in Christ. Believing this to be true, conducted in a private confession in Fr. Delma's office, I shared it all and cried uncontrollably the entire time. I was so sad and ashamed because I had done or failed to do so many things in my life that I couldn't even look Fr. Delma in the eye as I spoke. Once I was done confessing, Fr. Delma spoke the most amazing words to me. He softly said, "God sees you as beautiful." These few words brought relief and I could breathe again. Peace came and I believed God had readied me for the next part of my journey with Him.

Because Holy Saturday, the evening Mass before Easter Sunday, was the service when all R.C.I.A. members officially come into the Catholic Church, I decided to find the perfect new dress for this monumental occasion. My final selection was a pricey one in relationship to our family budget. Both Trista and Stephan got new clothes too because this was also their big moment to join the Church. Taking full advantage of the layaway programs, after four weeks we were paid up and duly outfitted.

It felt great to be in my new dress. I remember how the pale pink fabric was soft against my skin and the children looked incredibly proud of their new duds as we walked into the church to get direction from our instructors about what to do, when and how. Immediately, one of the teachers handed me a long robe to wear over my clothing for the Holy Saturday Mass. It occurred to me that God had a sense of humor because I had bought this new dress. This Mass couldn't be about the dress or how the dress made me feel. "I get it," I said to God as I smiled.

Receiving the Eucharist for the first time seemed like something I had been waiting for my whole life. Watching Trista and Stephan receive Jesus in this way brought me to tears. With Tara as their godmother as well as my sponsor, and our saints names ready in hand, we three were laid bare before the throne of God as innocents and in total awe of His greatness. Trista and Stephan, at nine and seven years of age, looked so beautiful and vulnerable. I know that none of us totally understood it all because it *is* a mystery. But for myself and as a parent, I surrendered who we were in exchange for who we would become in Christ. I prayed this way for the three of us as Steph looked on at his family.

I remember gazing on the large crucifix hanging above the altar, thinking about what Christ did for me and holding onto the small crucifix necklace I wore around my neck. Nearly nine months ago Fr. Glahn had charged me to take the classes and then ask the Holy Spirit what is truth. Truth was here and now. I was in love with Jesus and feeling so blessed that Christ the King was now our Church. Looking around, I realized that all these people were now my church family. We were home.

II Corinthians 6:2: "At the right time, I heard you. On the day of Salvation, I helped you. Indeed, God is ready to help you right now. Today is the day of salvation!"

So there we were, all four of us, regularly attending weekly Mass and making new church friends quickly. My husband began using his musical gifts to cantor the Mass and I occasionally sang with him. Our world of worship expanded in many new ways to learn about Christ, praise Him and serve Him.

CHAPTER 4

§

THE CHILDREN AND I HAD come into the Church at Easter of 1981 and by fall Steph and I were invited to attend a Catholic Cursillo which is a three-day cloistered retreat, a short course in Christianity. This retreat movement, created by a Catholic priest who noticed primarily only older women and children were attending weekly Mass, began in Spain nearly 20 years prior. Fr. Delma urged us to consider attending because many couples from church were planning to also attend and he was the lead spiritual director for the weekend. The schedule was that the men would attend their weekend first—Thursday evening through Sunday—then the women several weeks later. St. Stephan's Catholic Church in Owensboro was our retreat location where we would sleep on a gymnasium floor and have no watches so we would be completely on God's time. We were not permitted to communicate with the outside world nor the world to us, unless there was a true emergency. Since Tara, our children's godmother and my sponsor, also planned to attend, Steph and I agreed to go.

It was exciting and kind of "out there" for me to consider that we would be cloistered with about 42 other women for 72 hours with no distractions from the outside world. Steph attended his Cursillo Weekend but shared very little about what happened there. He did seem different, more calm, loving and at peace. I remember thinking that this retreat was a great idea! Who wouldn't want those characteristics in a spouse?

At the following Sunday Mass I observed that Steph had definitely bonded with the other men from our church who had also attended the retreat. It was a different type of bonding, demonstrated by big manly hugs, ear-to-ear grins and greetings with the peace of Christ. This was all new relationship territory for both of us. *Interesting*, I thought. *Will I be this way, too, after I attend the retreat?*

The day came to attend my women's Cursillo and Steph dropped me off at the instructed time. It was so good to see Tara's familiar face. I stood by her as we were told to form a long line across the wall on one side of the room. Methodically, as we introduced ourselves, we were assigned a table team—a group of six women—with whom we would more intimately experience the retreat when not in large-group activities. St. Cecelia, my table team's name, included one woman that I had seen at church, but barely knew. This weekend was an opportunity to get to know Velma, as well as to make new friends from other churches.

The weekend unfolded with lots of great food, laughing, talks given by both laywomen and clergy about various aspects of Christianity followed by table discussion. We were moving nicely into Friday afternoon when I realized that every single woman at the St. Cecelia table had experienced a terrible loss of someone—in either their immediate family or someone very close to them. Our table leader gave a talk about her husband passing away from a heart attack while their family was on a retirement cruise in a foreign country.

As trust grew and lives were shared, this beautiful, diverse St. Cecelia table group of women continued to tell their tragic stories. I felt very out of place because I had never experienced a death of someone close to me. My discomfort about this topic growing, I decided to confer with Fr. Delma about it and asked if I could switch to a different table team. In his usual gentle way he said "no," then explained that table teams were not randomly selected. He explained that after numerous people had invested much prayer, each retreat attendee was handpicked to be in a select table group. I trusted Fr.

Delma's decision and committed to continuing the rest of the retreat with the ladies of St. Cecelia's table. From this time on I mostly listened intently to their stories, trying to understand where they were coming from, although I struggled to relate to their personal stories about grief.

As a follow-up and continuation to the Cursillo Retreat weekend we were asked to become members of a Prayer and Share Group. This group would meet for one hour each week to keep sharing and growing in our faith. As directed, seven ladies who attended the retreat from our church formed a share group. We committed to meet each week at the home of our eldest member, Mary, so she wouldn't need to venture out in the evenings.

In these weekly faith-building get-togethers, the seven of us briefly shared, in total confidence, information requested on the official Prayer and Share Card given us at the conclusion of the retreat weekend. We prayed for each other and our love for each other and Jesus grew through the years of meeting together. These truly were my sisters in Christ. I trusted this beautiful, diverse group of women. God was using them to help me grow into a more mature faith. Because we held each other highly accountable to study, perform an act of service and give an honest account of our past week's behaviors, our time together served as a barometer of true faith in Christ.

Life was going well for us in Madisonville, Kentucky, and we were incredibly grateful. Our salon was thriving with a customer wait list. Steph's job at Goodyear seemed secure for our future and our new faith community was our venue of socialization for us and our children.

§

CHAPTER 5

IT WAS TIME FOR PUPPA and Grandma to visit us again from Akron and we could hardly wait to spend time with them, as always. In fact, we tried to get them to move to Kentucky. We believed we had a solid argument for the move since the two daughters lived only one house apart. Dad, although he loved us deeply, wouldn't hear of it. He envisioned that if he and Mom sold everything and left all they knew to move south, our husbands would be relocated and they would be stuck in Kentucky alone. I agreed this was a possibility although I believed we would likely live out our days in our current home and that would be great.

When my parents pulled into our driveway, our kids went crazy with excitement to be with them. Both Trista and young Stephan thoroughly enjoyed the special attention they got from my parents— from singing as Mom played the piano, to storytelling from my Dad. Again, each encounter was likely a lesson of some sort since that was my dad's MO.

In one such teaching moment, my dad decided to help Trista learn how to write a check. As she enthusiastically took pen in hand to complete information on the fake check Dad created, she was delighted to make payment in full for a purchase she was making. Because both Dad and Trista had beautiful cursive handwriting I couldn't wait to see Trista's series of completed checks for clothes, groceries and church offering. But something wasn't right. Dad made a funny facial expression as he noticed the information Trista attempted to put on the lines of the fake checks was not remotely on the lines. Some words were on top and some below the lines looking like a pre-schooler's writing who had struggled to stay within the allocated spaces. Concerned, Dad showed me the checks and we both agreed that Trista might need glasses since this writing was not normal for her.

Trista was thrilled with how she looked with her new frames and pranced around the house showing off a little with her hair in different looks to showcase her specs. But by the same token, we were totally perplexed to realize that even with her new glasses Trista's vision hadn't improved very much at all. She began to complain about headaches each morning and for several days in a row had gone to school with a headache. She even threw up at school but then felt better after about one o'clock in the afternoon. I decided it was time to take her to see our pediatrician.

"No need to be concerned," the doctor assured us. "Something at school must be worrying Trista to the point that she throws up," she said. Not agreeing at all with this conclusion because Trista was a straight A student who loved school, I was nonetheless relieved by our doctor's words. But the headaches continued, followed by an eruption of vomiting and by afternoon feeling fine. It was puzzling to us all.

My "mom intuition" began kicking into gear and I was suspecting something else was going on with our daughter. She seemed perfectly happy most of the time but now was getting tired very easily. Not feeling comfortable taking Trista back to her pediatrician, I asked one of my male hair clients, Dr. John Brewer, also a pediatrician, if he would agree to work Trista into his already busy schedule as a favor to me.

The next day it took all of five minutes for Dr. John Brewer to assess Trista's condition by identifying that a brain tumor was causing her vision to be impaired as it produced swelling in her optic nerve. Diagnosis was confirmed by an MRI/CAT scan. With tears in his eyes, Dr. John informed all three of us—Steph, Trista and me—that this was serious. We had no earthly idea how serious or how this information would impact our family.

Driving back to our house from the doctor's office, it was quiet in the car as I believe each of us was trying to process what Dr. Brewer had told us. After sharing the information with my mom and dad and young Stephan, we discussed how we would maneuver for Trista to be admitted to Vanderbilt University Children's Hospital in Nashville, a two hours' drive from our home. Scheduled for the following Monday morning to see Dr. Meecham, a renowned chief of Neurosurgery at this teaching facility, we had two days to create a plan.

In an instant our lives were changed. Reflecting on the fact that we second-mortgaged our home to build my dream salon, I wondered how we could make the payments without my income. I couldn't visualize how this could play out successfully. The fact was that we could lose our home. Always the practical and logistical family member, I asked one of our stylists at the salon if she would consider managing the business in my absence and I would pay her an additional $100 per week. Honestly, I wasn't sure where this would come from but I couldn't expect her to accept the added responsibility without any compensation. Marge was a detail person with a head for business and I trusted her completely. I was grateful she agreed to do it.

My sister Pam and my dear sister in Christ, Betty Walker, were set up to manage the reception area in my absence. The salon staff, that included Tara, really rallied to the occasion to plan how they would continue to work to keep the salon in the black. I couldn't imagine this even possible for very long. But losing everything wasn't as concerning to me as Trista's illness. My priorities were to get my daughter well and home as quickly as possible. All else: Well, those chips would need to fall where they may.

My Prayer and Share Group was truly there for our family, praying with us, for us and offering to do whatever was needed. Our faith community at church prayed over Trista the Sunday before we left for Nashville. Their prayers strengthened me and I didn't feel as alone on this journey as I had when we first heard the news in the doctor's office.

CHAPTER 6

§

THE MORNING ARRIVED FOR US to leave for Nashville and the four of us piled into the car to hit the road. Until we knew what we were up against, we decided we needed to be together. Very generously, Mom and Dad decided to stay at our house until we had more information about the plan to treat Trista.

Funny, I always thought of Nashville, Tennessee, as the music city capital of the world, the home of country stars, never the location for treating a child's brain tumor. Fear gripped me as we drove up to the hospital, but I wouldn't let anyone see me cry. I was not going to panic. Besides, it might not be all that bad and I did believe that God could do anything. *God is in control*, I thought to myself, a thought that calmed me down to be able to have a peaceful demeanor for my family.

The Vanderbilt Children's team was highly seasoned about how to initiate families, such as us, into this medical culture. In a spirit of kindness and consideration, the registrant swiftly checked us in and asked Trista to get into a wheelchair so we could get her to her hospital room. I could see the fear on Trista's face as the attendant took the helm of the wheelchair to move her across the glossy floor. As we entered her room, Trista was helped onto the bed and we were told that a nurse would be with us shortly to provide more information. The attendant hadn't cleared the doorway out of her room when Trista turned her head toward me like a bullet, looked me squarely in the eyes and said, "Mom, promise me that you will never leave me." I gave my word not knowing if I could totally live up to my promise.

The nurse did arrive soon and she was as kind and joyful as all the others we had met so far. Her recommendation was that the three of us check into the Ronald McDonald House for several days since Trista was on the schedule for surgery in two days. Tears welled up in Trista's eyes at about the same time I eyeballed the window seat in this fifth-floor private room. I asked the nurse if I could sleep there so that I could keep the promise I made to Trista minutes earlier. Promising she would check on that for us, it wasn't long before it was approved. Trista was relieved and so was I.

Trista and I got settled into her room and later our guys, Steph and Stephan, ended up staying at a hotel that several men from our church had arranged for them since the Ronald McDonald house was full. My mom and dad, as well as Steph's parents, planned to arrive the next day to be at the hospital for surgery scheduled for the following day. In their complete candor, the surgeons, Dr. Meecham and the attending resident Dr. Rigsby, informed us that Trista might not survive the surgery, or she might be permanently physically impaired. Another possibility was that she could go into a coma or might not have complete mental capacity to know us. There was no way to know the exact outcome until after the surgery but they did their best to prepare us for possible outcomes.

An unexpected cheery note to our late afternoon came when a cute, shorthaired woman in a nurse's uniform peeked into our doorway to say "hello." It was Allison Bolin, a woman whose hair I had done on occasion back in Madisonville. She explained that her Aunt Tony, who was one of my regular salon clients, told her we would be here and to look us up if she had time. It seems that Allison had moved to Nashville to be on the Vanderbilt Life Flight Team. It was truly comforting to know we had a friend in the building and Allison assured us she would be checking on us regularly.

As evening came, Trista and I picked up that something was going on in the hospital on our floor. We saw nurses scurrying around and there was giggling, laughing. Unable to withstand the suspense, I peeked out the door of our room and asked a nurse what was going on. "Another miracle!" she said. "What do you mean?" I asked. She then told us that a young boy was scheduled for a serious surgery in a couple of days. This little boy and his parents, believing in God's healing power, asked that the doctor run one more test before the surgery to be certain the boy needed it. The test concluded without question that the cancerous tumor was gone, completely gone. No one could explain how, but it was nowhere to be seen on the test and his family was going home.

Trista and I pondered this news in silence but we both must have been thinking the same thing. If God could heal this boy, He most certainly could heal Trista. I pointed out to Trista what also stood out to me about what the nurse had said. She clearly said, "Another miracle." I loved the sound of those words and it was a gift to know that this sometimes really happens. There could be a miracle for us. All things are possible with God and we knew that.

That first night in the hospital Trista and I heard a lot of commotion in the room right next door. Then we heard wailing and loud crying. Our nurse knew we had heard and that I would ask so she came into our room to let us know that the little girl next door, who had been in a coma for a very long time, just died. Thinking Trista would be as terrified as I was to hear such news, I scrambled to think of what to say to her once the nurse left the room. But Trista spoke first, in order to comfort me, I think, when she said, "Jenny isn't hurting anymore." There was nothing more to say and so we quietly went to sleep, I on my window seat and she in her hospital bed with the rails pulled up.

§

CHAPTER 7

MORNING CAME AND EVERYONE SPENT the day in our room. Young Stephan had many questions but he also managed to make us laugh by performing a little break-dancing for us. By dinner, both sets of grandparents left so that the four of us could have some private family time. We all prayed and silently I asked for a miracle like the one the little boy had experienced the day before so that Trista wouldn't need her surgery either. Then our guys left the room heading to the hotel for the night.

Sleep never came to Trista or me. Although never spoken aloud, we both knew that this could be our last night together and we certainly did not intend to spend these few hours sleeping. We talked about all kinds of things. Trista asked questions, many of which I simply could not answer. As I sat beside her bed holding her hand, she made me promise that no matter what happened, I would always tell her the truth about her condition. I gave her my word.

We were quiet for what seemed like a very long time when Trista suddenly burst out crying and said she was afraid. I cried right along with her, partly because I couldn't take this cancer or surgery from her and partly because there were no words of mine that could change this situation. It was frightening for us both. Just as suddenly as she had begun crying earlier, she quit crying, looked at the window and started to smile. It was a big smile like one of those when the smiling person knows an important something you don't.

It was dark outside as it usually is in the middle of the night. We were on the fifth floor of the hospital, plus Trista had lost a major portion of her vision. I thought, *What in the world was she looking at in that window?*

Trista then whispered very softly, "Mom, do you see that woman in the window?" "No," I said. Trista then went on to tell me that the woman in the window was wearing a beautiful blue dress and no shoes. I listened but saw nothing! Trista giggled out loud, but then grew quiet and calm. "What's going on?" I asked softly while I was trying desperately to see what she was clearly seeing. The lady in the window had a message for her, Trista shared. "Don't be afraid. I won't ever leave you. I'll always be with you." As Trista and I both began to cry, I realized who was in the window. Tears this time were ones of excitement and great joy. Trista really wasn't afraid after the Blessed Mother came to see her. She wasn't ever afraid again.

Some people may read this, discount this visitation, and attribute it to medication. But Trista wasn't on any medication. Even if she had been, I believed Trista who was never prone to imaginary friends or embellishing in any way. I knew it was true and believed it! What other explanation could there be for my child to one minute be hysterically frightened and moments later be at total peace about her impending surgery. *I* couldn't even pull that off.

I began to visualize the surgical room tomorrow morning where I could not go with Trista. I could see the Mother of our Lord standing beside my daughter. What comfort that gave me! I believed that Trista would be fine, be healed, in fact. This visitation was so encouraging. We were not alone at all.

CHAPTER 8

§

MORNING DID COME AND ONCE again the extended family gathered at Trista's bedside to pray before attendants took Trista to surgery. No one cried or was sad and Trista seemed just fine with it all, even when the resident came into the room to explain step-by-step what they would be doing during surgery to remove the tumor and what to expect for a recovery process post-surgery. The graphic and horrific description of the procedure to remove the tumor was surreal to me. It was like we were all in a bad movie—one I would never want to see. I couldn't grasp this would really happen to my 12-year-old child. Then I remembered Our Lady's words and peace came once again.

We all kissed Trista good-bye and a very kind and caring nurse wheeled Trista away.

Because Trista was probably going to be in intensive care for several days after surgery, we had to give up her current room. All belongings had to be removed immediately. After completing this task, we headed to the surgical waiting room where the balance of the family was waiting for us. Minutes seemed like hours and hours like days as we began to play potential scenarios out in our heads about what it would be like with each outcome described by our doctors—death, coma, paralysis, conscious without knowing us anymore. Every option gave birth to a different set of concerns in my mind as I went over each one again and again. This went on until

I was exhausted from all the thinking, as I remembered that Trista and I had been up all night talking.

I watched as my husband wandered away from where our family was seated because he had spotted a lone man who appeared so down in spirit he was openly crying with his head in his hands. Steph approached the man and sat next to him. The man looked dirty and even from where I sat I could smell him. After Steph asked if he could help the man, the lonely stranger shared that his daughter was in surgery and that there was no one to wait with him during this most grueling time. I'm not sure what conversation was exchanged between the two men but I do know that my husband prayed with this man and that made me cry.

Just to set the scene for you in the waiting room: My parents and Steph's parents came from two different planets in regard to their ideologies and approaches to life. Although Steph and all his siblings attended private Catholic schools through grade twelve, Steph's dad hadn't believed in God since WWII when he served as a paratrooper and witnessed so much destruction and disregard for human life. Whereas, my parents were very involved in church and lived a vibrant Christian faith. My mom served as the Christian Education Director of a large Presbyterian church in Akron for years. My sister Pam and I practically lived at the church and we loved all the activities, service work and family commitment to worship each week. This said, my father-in-law and mother-in-law loved their six children, were incredibly kind and generous to us and had driven down to Nashville from Akron just to be with us as support.

Steph's dad, trying to break the painful silence by initiating interaction with my parents, asked my dad if cancer ran in our family. Dad shared that my mom had recovered from breast cancer and that he had an incident, although cleared for many years, with prostate cancer. To this, Steph's dad confirmed confidently that there had never been any cancer in his family that he had been aware of. So Trista's cancer may have come from the Stewart side.

I know that my father-in-law had no malicious intent, but that last comment ended any hope for additional civil discussion between the two sets of parents. There was no more exchange of conversation from either set of parents from then on. Although this last conversation was an interesting diversion for me, I couldn't go there at that time. The whole thing was still like watching a movie with characters such as the smelly man, my parents and Steph's parents. The time dragged on and on.

I remembered watching an episode of *The Twilight Zone* where a man named Tim had died and was waiting in an outer room with many other people. Tim was told that at the proper time his name would be called and he would learn where he would spend all of eternity, heaven or hell.

Growing weary and annoyed with the other people who were waiting with him and exasperated by one man who kept showing home movies of his family which included a ridiculous amount of commentating to explain the details, Tim was more than ready to get out of there and simply to be told his eternal fate. In his impatience, Tim knocked on the door to the inner room and asked how much longer it would be before his name would be called. He said he couldn't stand waiting with these horrible stupid people and they were all making him crazy. The voice behind the door responded to Tim's question by saying, "Tim, your name will never be called. Staying in this room with these people is your hell for all eternity." The voice behind the door laughed loudly as the viewer watched Tim fearfully gasp while facing the camera.

To me, hell would certainly include spending an inordinate amount of time waiting outside a surgical unit not knowing whether your child would live or die, be disabled, in a coma or know your face. I closed my eyes and remembered the Blessed Mother, asking her to take care of Trista in there as she had promised, to not let her die or lose her beautiful personality. Not long after this prayer, the doors swung open and Dr. Meecham gave us the report that the tumor was successfully removed. He explained that they didn't yet know the extent of the damage incurred and wouldn't know until she woke up. But, she was alive; she had survived the surgery. Praise God!

We all hugged, thanked Dr. Meecham and I took a deep breath as I thanked the Blessed Mother.

Knowing that Trista survived the surgery and that a promising recovery was projected, the grandparents headed back north to their respective residences in Akron while Steph and son Stephan went back to Madisonville for work and school. Our family plan was to keep life as normal as possible, committing to personally connect each day so that I could keep everyone abreast of Trista's progress.

CHAPTER 9

§

BECAUSE I NOW HAD NO window seat in a hospital room and could only visit Trista for 15-minute intervals, I decided not to say anything to the nursing staff about my plan to snooze on the waiting-room couch outside the Intensive Care Unit (ICU). This way, I would be available to be with my daughter at a moment's notice. The nurses likely knew my plan and looked the other way to allow it. They couldn't have been more kind or helpful by what they did and didn't do.

By early evening, Trista still hadn't woken up so I decided this would be a good time to call home and check in. What Steph shared with me on the phone blew me away. My Prayer and Share Group of ladies, in our absence, had cleaned our entire house and made enough food for the week, which was already in the refrigerator and freezer. They informed Steph that their commitment to our family was to continue this service every week when Steph and Stephan came to visit us on the weekends as long as Trista was at Vanderbilt.

I would like to note here that all of these women were married, had children and their own homes to maintain plus their own family's meals to cook every day. I cried, especially when I considered that my guys were not that neat in their day–to–day routines, especially in the bathrooms. This thought struck horror in me as I realized someone was cleaning around those commodes. So I called one of the ladies in the group—Cheryl—to find out who was doing this particular task. Reluctant to tell me at first, she said, "That would be me." I shared how sorry I was that she should have done such a task. She stopped me mid-sentence to tell me that it was a privilege. Of course, I cried while wondering if I would volunteer to do such a job for someone else and would I see it as an honor or privilege.

My next phone call was to check on things at the salon. Marge, our acting salon manager, and sister Pam said all was well and running smoothly so I headed back to my couch outside the ICU to wait for Trista to wake up from surgery. I began wondering if Marge or Pam would have told me if things weren't going well at the salon. But I couldn't let my mind go there right now. Keep in mind that there weren't any cell phones in the 1980's and every call cost a lot of money. I tried to keep calls short and sweet and I planned what to say before calling to be most concise.

It wasn't long before the nurse peeked her head around the entrance to the ICU and looking around to find me, called my name, "Mrs. France, Trista is waking up. You can come on in." Afraid because there was still that chance she might not know me, I slowly approached her bed, making sure I didn't touch any of the many cords attached to her. Her head, wound tightly in a big bandage, seemed to squeeze her head. It looked so tight and she looked so sweet, so young, so vulnerable lying there. Tears came to my eyes just seeing her and remembering the surgical process she had gone through. Opening her eyes slightly and then all the way, she looked at me, "Mom." Praise God she knew me. Although groggy, we talked for a few minutes until the nurse returned to give me some insight about her medication. She explained that Trista would be on high doses of steroids to keep the swelling down in her head and that this would make her highly sensitive to touch. I couldn't even hear what the nurse was saying. I knew that my little girl knew me, her mom, and I was thankful for that. Anything else, we would deal with as it occurred. All that was important now was that Trista was alive and she was still Trista!

When the nurse alerted me that my 15 minutes with Trista had ended I went back to the couch outside the ICU. I was so tired and realized I had nothing left in me. Being up for over 24 hours was finally catching up with me. Once I heard the name, "Mom," spoken to me, I relaxed like a rag doll. Looking out the window I could see it was dark, which triggered my body to sink onto that couch for a peaceful and restful sleep.

It seemed like I had only been sleeping minutes when I heard a noise near me. Checking my watch, it was about three A.M. Looking to my immediate left, still half groggy from my deep sleep, I saw a man who was barely able to stand. He urinated onto the carpet near the couch as though he were at a urinal. Getting my full wits about me, I jumped off the couch and located a hospital security guard I had seen in the hall earlier who promptly escorted the man out of the area while he radioed a maintenance man to clean up the mess.

Under normal conditions, this incident would have horrified and frightened me, but for some reason it didn't at all. This man had not even seen me on the couch and didn't know I was there. This was not about me but rather about a poor, inebriated soul who wandered undetected into the hospital and to this floor. He was simply relieving himself. I laid right back down on a nearby couch and fell back to sleep as though nothing had happened.

The second time I was allowed to see Trista for 15 minutes she was far more alert. And although she was on morphine for pain, was pretty uncomfortable. A nurse who seemed very tired and in a big hurry entered Trista's room to draw some of her blood. After the second unsuccessful attempt to hit a vein, Trista started to cry and said that it really hurt. This nurse's response to Trista threw me for a loop when she said, "Quit being such a big baby." At this point I totally lost it, stood and responded, "You leave this room now and never come back!" I could hear the nurses bustling around behind the curtain that separated Trista's section from the other patients and it wasn't any time at all until another nurse entered our space carrying the equipment necessary to draw blood and was holding the order in her hand. She explained that she was part of the special children's IV team and would appreciate the opportunity to draw

Trista's blood. She asked Trista if she could have one try. Trista agreed and the nurse was true to her word.

I began to think about all the children who could experience similar disastrous situations regarding unkind medical service providers with no advocate in their rooms. I thanked God I was there with Trista, and then said a prayer for all the other children in ICU.

CHAPTER 10

§

AFTER THREE DAYS IN ICU, Trista was taken back to a real hospital room where I once again took up residence on the window seat
cushion. Praise God that all was going so well except for one thing.
Trista had lost the use of one leg and the other one was very weak.
One arm that had been weak before surgery was more weakened and
her blindness had worsened. Still so very grateful she was alive and
herself, we agreed that we were going to thank God for what we had
and not dwell on what was gone.

Weaned from the morphine but still on high doses of steroids,
Trista was her beautiful and precocious self, only she seemed to have
more energy with a giddy sort of happiness that I learned later can be
side-effects of prednisone. I remember thinking, "I'm totally okay
with those side-effects!"

CHAPTER 11

§

A WEEK HAD GONE BY and Steph and Stephan could finally return to be with us for a bit. We were thrilled because there was a possibility that Trista would be able to sit in a wheelchair for a short time so we could get her out of the room. I'm sure that by this time, she was pretty tired of just me.

When Steph and Stephan arrived in the room they were thrilled to see Trista so alert and happy. Stephan made us all laugh at every opportunity and what a blessing that was for all of us to laugh together. Just as the nurse had predicted, Trista was able to be in a wheelchair for a short while and we headed for the children's playroom. While in the elevator, on the way down to the correct floor, the elevator stopped and a doctor got on. In the elevator was our family of four and this young doctor who Trista could not see because of her blindness. Once the elevator door closed, a very foul odor permeated the elevator. Because Trista was her "real" self she said loudly, "Okay, who had the gas? Euwee!" After turning bright red and clearly anxious for the elevator door to open onto his floor, the young doctor scrambled quickly through the door. We all cracked up in laughter so that tears were running down our faces. Once Steph, Stephan and I were able to stop laughing, we told Trista the deal and she laughed, too. God gives us the gift of laughter and I was grateful for this moment that I cherish to this day. I'm certain that God sent that young unsuspecting doctor to us so we could have a giant laugh at his expense. Whoever he was, God bless him!

Once we made it to the children's playroom Trista couldn't see clearly, so she listened a lot and then asked us to describe what was happening. Young Stephan couldn't wait to give her the full scoop from his perspective. His interpretations were thoroughly entertaining for us. I'll never forget seeing children so disabled and impaired in various ways, yet they were playing and laughing as though they didn't realize they had any problems at all. It occurred to me that these children were easily entertained and that this was a special place. Both Trista and Stephan agreed that the music being played while we were there was, as they described it, "lame," since they were more into artists such as Michael Jackson. It was such a treat to be in a different environment with all four of us together again.

Since we couldn't keep Trista sitting up in the wheelchair very long, we headed back to her room so she could lie down and get some rest. Our two guys left for a little while but came back later with McDonald's burgers and fries which we all inhaled quickly. It was such a wonderful day and we were so thankful. It was now time for Steph and Stephan to head back home. We said our good-byes, assured that these few precious hours would sustain us all until the next visit.

§

CHAPTER 12

THE NURSE HAD EXPLAINED TO me that Trista's hair would likely fall out and at the time I didn't give it much thought. However, the day came that Trista could run her fingers through her hair and remove giant clumps from all around her partially bandaged head. The cause may have been the steroids she was on. Trista found this to be great fun. With large clumps of hair in her hand, she would laugh and hand it off to me to throw away and then dig in for the next clump. Thank God she couldn't clearly see the expression on my face as she handed me her hair because for some reason it horrified me. I had seen pictures of those bald-headed children on television when charities were asking for donations for cancer research. That bald-headed child was my daughter. It was now about my family. Cancer had come to our house and was changing our lives forever.

Once Trista was satisfied she had pulled out all remaining hair she could get to, she decided to take a nap. Slipping quietly from her room I headed downstairs to the lobby to call my sister, Pam. It was a lengthy call—not typical for me—but the only thing I said was, "Trista's hair just came out," after which I held the phone to my ear and cried uncontrollably until I said that I had to go back to the room. Why that phone call made me feel better, I'm not sure, but it did, and then all I could think of was that I was ready for Trista to recover so we could go home to Kentucky.

CHAPTER 13

§

IN SPITE OF ALL THE craziness that goes along with such a traumatic life shift, after weeks in the hospital, Steph and Stephan visiting on the weekends, Trista and I started to get into a bit of a routine about how we spent our days. In this groove, the new normal, Trista's spirits were consistently high and I noticed she was starting to develop a little crush on her young neurosurgeon resident, Dr. Rigsby. Also, during this time, Trista and I spent a lot of time praying for people, saying the Rosary and singing a lot together. My parents loved to sing and they had taught Trista all the old Baptist hymns I had learned as a kid such as, *When the Roll is Called up Yonder* and *There is a Fountain*. Things could be much *worse*, I thought. It seemed like everything would be all right once we got home. We both looked forward to that day.

After several more weeks had passed, Trista started getting a bit frustrated that we couldn't go home, so she began asking the doctors every day if today was the day. And every day they asked her to be patient. Finally, Trista's resident heartthrob agreed to order her a CAT scan so he could check the area of her brain where the tumor had been removed.

We were totally unprepared for the outcome of that test. The tumor had already grown back and was now growing even more aggressively than before. Her doctors recommended a second surgery be performed immediately. Because Trista was so eager to go home and clearly needed a break, the doctors agreed to let us go home over the weekend. We would then need to check back in for the surgery to be performed on the following Monday.

CHAPTER 14

§

IT WAS SO GOOD TO be home—despite the dread of what might be ahead. My Prayer and Share group had the house looking better than I could have. In fact, the ladies were still there when we arrived. It was quite a welcome-home gift.

The weekend went by quickly, especially on Sunday starting with Mass. Our church family prayed over Trista and I knew that their prayers would be ongoing. Tara, Trista's godmother, came to see her and before we knew it, it was time for the guys, Steph and Stephan, to take us back to Nashville. Arrangements were made for them to stay at a hotel near the hospital out of the generosity of fellow Christ the King parishioners.

The process and procedure were planned to be the same as before, as were the projected risks, but the neurosurgeons were encouraging. We prayed for a miracle like the one we heard about when we first arrived at Vanderbilt. "God can do anything," I said to myself.

The night before this second scheduled surgery, Trista slept well. Maybe this was because she knew what to expect and she remembered what the Blessed Mother had said to her from the fifth-floor window of her previous room. Me, I couldn't sleep or even rest. I begged God for healing, not just survival from surgery, but for a healing so complete that we could go back to the life that we had before Trista was sick. In my selfishness, I wanted it to be over or to simply wake up from this horrible dream. This had gone on too long.

During the second surgery to remove the second brain tumor, only our immediate family was at the hospital. Since we now had a frame of reference for the amount of time Trista might be in surgery, Steph, Stephan and I spent the waiting time talking to each other and snacking often, mostly to help young Stephan, now ten years old, have something to do. Waiting, even sitting still for very long, was always tough on him. It was for all of us.

Since Stephan had become familiar with the hospital environment, where the bathrooms were, where to go for snacks, we gave him some freedom to walk around the area where we waited. We asked that he check in with us frequently. It was during one of those independent jaunts that a door separating one unit from another, was about to close on him before he was totally through the doorway. Thinking these hospital doors were similar to the elevator doors that would open up when the sensor detected an object was obstructing the entrance, Stephan proceeded through the door while attempting to keep the door open with his left hand. This was how he came to break his finger.

It all got pretty interesting for our family at this time since I needed to take Stephan to the ER for treatment while Steph took up residence in the surgical waiting room in case Dr. Meecham or Dr. Rigsby came looking for us.

As crazy as this sounds, Stephan breaking his finger was a good and important thing to happen. My beautiful son may have needed my undivided attention, even for a short while. I probably needed that, too.

I began to consider how little one-on-one time my son and I had spent together and I missed that. He and I had a very special relationship and I was likely going to continue to be missing out on the day-to-day events in his life—the little victories, the challenges, the talks we liked to have while sitting on his bed in his room. He and I had always been close, maybe because he seemed to need me more than Trista did before she got sick. For one thing, Stephan had to work harder for his grades. Although he was curious and smart, he was also a ball of energy and it was challenging to keep him engaged on one topic for very long. But he had and still does have, a loving, sensitive personality combined with a very creative spirit. Each of our children was so very unique and beautiful to me. Each needed different things from me. Trista needed me to never leave her as she battled for her very life while Stephan, as a young man approaching adolescence, needed me to be physically and emotionally present to help him walk through this challenging time in his life.

CHAPTER 15

§

ANOTHER MIRACLE--AND WE SURE NEEDED it! Praise God the surgery went well. The tumor was successfully removed for the second time. Again we wouldn't know the extent of any potential residual damage until she regained consciousness in the ICU. Encouraged, though, Steph and Stephan hit the road for the two-hour drive back to Madisonville so they could get back to work and school respectively.

Since I saw evidence that security had been beefed up a notch since I last sat outside ICU, I felt confident that there wouldn't be any more incidents of inebriated men needing to urinate anywhere around me this time. I slept, in fact, so deeply that the ICU nurse had to shake me to fully wake me for my 15-minute visit with Trista who had regained consciousness and was asking for her mom.

From the very first day Trista and I arrived at Vanderbilt, Trista asked if she could wear the small gold crucifix necklace that Steph had bought me in Scotland while we were on our family trip several years prior to this. She loved rubbing her hands over the cross and feeling the details of the body of Jesus with her fingers while her eyes were closed. I watched her do this often and I'm sure it gave her great comfort. It did me, also, just watching her. So, when Trista was coming out of anesthesia and asked for the necklace back, I was incredibly thankful and again encouraged. Praise God, Trista is still Trista! Thank you, Lord!

CHAPTER 16

§

AFTER SPENDING SEVERAL DAYS IN ICU, the ICU nurse informed us that the doctors had ordered a CAT scan to be performed on Trista before she would be released back to a regular hospital room. The nurse also reminded us that Trista would need to be able to urinate on her own within the next few hours since the catheter had been removed earlier in the day. The deal was that if Trista was unable to urinate on her own, the catheter would need to be reinserted. This was terrifying to Trista. Before the nurse had even taken two steps out of our area, Trista's eyes opened very wide and she began to cry. Because she was on high doses of steroids to keep the swelling down inside her head, her skin had become super sensitive, which she explained to me meant catheterization was excruciatingly painful when she was conscious. Her skin had become so sensitive that to even hug Trista caused her great discomfort. After discussing this new development, she decided that our new hugging protocol would be for me to lean near her and she would hug me as she felt comfortable to do. This worked well for her.

Distracted from Trista's catheterization fears, a uniformed hospital transportation staff person arrived to take Trista to X-ray. Being very familiar with the process requiring all metal to be removed from the patient, Trista removed the crucifix necklace and handed it to me for safekeeping. Fastening it around my own neck as I followed behind her wheelchair, I finished the lengthy walk and then sat and waited outside the X-ray area. On occasion Trista appreciated the opportunity to do things on her own. Now 13 years old, I think her "teenage" exercises for practicing independence became apparent more frequently. Trista typically acted and generally shared thoughts that seemed to me far beyond the maturity of a normal young woman her age, even before she got sick. Respecting her wishes, I waited outside the X-ray unit or stayed behind whenever she needed her "space."

The CAT scan didn't take long. It wasn't any time at all before Trista was comfortably back in the ICU bed when she asked for the necklace back. After reaching to find the clasp on the chain around my neck, I couldn't believe that the chain wasn't there at all. Not wanting to freak Trista out, I began quickly looking all around the area near her bed, my chair, anywhere it might have fallen. After tracing all of my steps and alerting the nurses to be on the lookout, I had no choice but to tell Trista I couldn't find the necklace. "Then we've got to pray for help to find it," she said rather curtly to me. So we did and Trista cried the entire time. "O God, please help us find this necklace. It is so important to us. We love you. We trust you. Please show us where it is," as she continually cried through the words. Still, no necklace appeared.

Nurses were kind to put the word out and to ask other parents to be on the lookout for the necklace, but no necklace presented itself. Meanwhile, time was quickly running out for Trista to prove that she could urinate on her own.

I asked Trista to please try to urinate in the bedpan, but she just kept crying while explaining that she was sure that there wasn't anything in there to get out. She drank more water. We talked about rivers flowing. I went to the bathroom and was explaining in great detail how relieving that felt when the nurse stepped back into the room with the catheter in hand. The second Trista heard her voice she begged her for more time. "Just give me 15 minutes more. I know I'll go. Please!" After reluctantly granting Trista an extension, the nurse explained that she would be back in 15 minutes.

Trista was in gear to pray like I'd never seen her pray before. She said, "Mom, beg God to let me go potty. Beg Him, I'm running out of time." We prayed together and then I planned to step away to pray for her in the bathroom because I was so angry with God and I didn't want her to hear the conversation I planned to have with Him about the missing crucifix necklace and Trista's inability to urinate. I was ticked! I told Trista that I would be right back.

After I closed the thick bathroom door, my prayer to God, if you could call it a prayer, went something like this: "Are you kidding me, God? Enough! This child has been through so much. She needs you to do such a simple thing for her. You can do anything! I know that. Please let her go potty and then locate the necklace. We need you *RIGHT* now! Hurry, Lord, before the nurse comes back. Oh God, now!"

When I stepped back into the room near Trista's bed, the nurse walked in right behind me with "the kit" and said that time was up. This wasn't said in a cruel way, but rather a very caring way as she explained that it was dangerous for Trista not to be able to release her urine. Both Trista and I knew the nurse didn't want to hurt her. Then Trista asked the nurse if she would help her to the bathroom because she knew she could go once she was in there. Again, very reluctantly, the nurse agreed. Sure enough, Trista did go! Praise God! "Thank you Jesus," I said out loud. "Thank you, Jesus," Trista shouted even louder. At this the nurse laughed with us. Praise God! To this very day, whenever I go to the bathroom, I thank God for this gift of being able to go. It is a blessing to be able to go to the bathroom on your own. Not everyone can do that, you know.

CHAPTER 17

§

RELEASED FROM ICU AND FINALLY back in a regular hospital room once again, I quickly got set up in my spot in the window seat. Trista shared that she was getting tired. It had been quite an ordeal and I'm sure she was exhausted from the trauma of the great catheter challenge so we both agreed to hit the sack early. ICU is not the most restful place with lights, constant scurrying of nurses plus all the sounds of devices from which one may be monitored. After helping Trista into a clean gown and teeth brushing, I decided to take a quick shower. It had been a very long day. It was relieving just to be finally free of the confines of my bra. As I was placing it onto my clothes pile, I spied the crucifix necklace inside one of the cups of my bra. Sobbing in thanksgiving to God, I stepped out of the bathroom and placed it back around Trista's neck where it belonged. I watched her close her eyes when she felt the tiny body of Christ on the cross with her fingers. I knew Christ was with us. We were at peace. He had never left us.

As exhausted as I was that night, after my quick shower I prayed the Rosary, The Lord's Prayer and just kept thanking God. I'm not sure when, I fell sound asleep.

§

CHAPTER 18

Since Trista had first been diagnosed with brain cancer, I hadn't given much thought about our family finances at all. Whenever I checked on the salon solvency, Marge, acting manager, reported that all was going well and when I asked Steph about how our personal finances were going, he'd explain that he was working as much as he could to keep up with the bills. In an effort not to give me anything else to be concerned about, he didn't let me know that our savings were totally wiped out. He was operating the family budget on such a low balance that there was no extra money to spend on anything at all. None!

Because I had always been our family financial manager, I decided it was time to get a more specific read about our financial status from our bank. I was shocked to learn that our checking account had little money left. I wondered how Steph and Stephan were managing to buy groceries or even gas for the car to come see us.

It had been my practice to cash a check at the hospital each week for $20 so I could buy my food and have meals eating with Trista on her schedule. Eating mostly comfort food, the extra carbs had really spiked my weight gain but it didn't concern me at the time. *One thing at a time*, I thought. I ate whenever Trista ate. If she was hungry for dessert, I enjoyed something sweet right along with her.

The stark reality now was that there was no more money. I couldn't keep taking $20 out each week when I knew that Steph and Stephan were attempting to live on so little. I decided that from now on I would simply eat whatever Trista couldn't finish on her tray. She usually ate pretty well but at this time wasn't a big eater. There was always some food left. Besides, I needed to get those extra pounds off and this seemed like a logical plan for me to lose some weight.

For several weeks I was living out my new eating- and financial-frugality plan. I really didn't feel any worse for having done this. Free coffee was always available in the visitor's lobby so I would go help myself to that fairly often. Realizing I was beginning to lose some significant weight, I was proud of myself for coming up with such a great solution on my own without worrying Steph or the rest of the family.

Early one morning, Trista's nurse walked in the room and took note that I was blowing my nose a lot and asked if I was getting a cold. Telling her that I wasn't sure, she explained that if I did get a cold, I wouldn't be able to sleep in Trista's room anymore. Trista's resistance to infection was low and we couldn't risk her getting a cold or any infection. The nurse then also said that I looked like I had lost some weight and again asked if I was okay. After assuring her that I was fine on both observations, she asked what I had been eating lately because she hadn't seen me coming or going into the room with any cafeteria food. After assuring her a third time that I was doing fine, the nurse left to continue her morning rounds.

I remember that this was an emotional low point for me. I thought I had been pretty clever to figure out what to do about having no money and little food to eat. But it wasn't really working if I had to leave Trista because I got sick as a result. Trista was napping and I had to get out of the hospital for a little while to think this through. I thought that maybe the fresh air would be good for me since I hadn't been able to leave the building or even breathe fresh outside air in a long time. So, out the front door I went, like I knew where I was going. But I certainly did not. After walking for who knows how long, I noticed a little sports bar which was a venue totally out of character for me to frequent. But then again, everything about our lives was totally out of the norm. *What the heck is norm?* I thought.

So I walked into the door of the bar like I'd been there many times and took a seat on a stool at the long counter, which was facing the bartender. Service being exceptional, the female bartender asked what I needed. *Great question*, I thought. I explained that I had no money, my child was in recovery from brain cancer and I just needed a change of scenery to think. Smiling back at me as though nothing I said phased her cheery spirit in the least, again she asked, "What could I get you?" "An orange juice would be perfect," I said.

I sipped that orange juice ever so slowly and watched the people eating, drinking, going about their day. They laughed, whispered to each other and didn't seem to have a care in the world except deciding what they would order. It felt good to be there among these people who looked like business professionals for the most part. Nevertheless, it was time for me to get back to my reality before Trista woke up. Thanking the bartender, I shook her hand and she squeezed my hand tightly in response.

The tears streamed slowly down my face as I upped the pace back toward the hospital. The faster I walked the harder I cried because I still didn't know what to do to get money for food to be healthy for Trista. I had given my word that I would never leave her. "God help me. I don't have anything left," I said under my breath as I walked back through the hospital lobby.

As I stepped back into Trista's room she was just waking up and hadn't even noticed I'd been gone. I was grateful at this moment that her vision was so poor so that she couldn't tell I had been crying. Just then the same nurse who had spoken to me earlier about potentially having a cold and about my weight loss, stepped into Trista's room and asked to see me in the hall for a minute. Thinking she probably wanted to give me a message from the doctors or had an update I needed to know about, I quickly followed her from the room. For a second I had a frightening thought that this nurse may think I looked worse than when she saw me last and would make me leave Trista's room. *O God, please*, I thought. *Help me. I don't want to leave my daughter and I have no place else to go.*

In a voice that was so gentle and kind, the nurse whispered, "You can cash a check with me personally so you'll have money for food." I burst out crying and then told her that would be impossible because a check of any amount would likely bounce. She gave me a rather strange look and then abruptly said she would see me later because a patient needed her right then.

It was grueling thinking about what the nurse would say to me when she got back, but I had no choice but to wait. Trista and I spent the rest of the afternoon talking and resting.

At five P.M. I heard the dinner cart coming down the hall right on schedule. Trista and I jumped the gun a little and thanked God for the meal before the food was actually delivered to her room. Seconds later, the meal delivery lady arrived carrying in two dinner trays. I explained to the woman that there must be some mistake because Trista had a private room. The woman checked her delivery chart and gave me a testy look as though I had offended her professionalism. She then sharply turned her tiny body toward me indignantly and said, "No mistake. This room gets two trays." Off she went toward the hall to continue on-time delivery to the next room on her list.

Moments later, in walked Trista's nurse who looked me straight in the eyes and abruptly said, "Don't ask. See you two later and, by the way, here's a little something to help you get rid of those sniffles. I'm sure it's just allergies." Smiling kindly, she walked out.

At this, I had to go to the bathroom, shut the door and cry for a while to thank God for what He had done for me. I ate and was grateful for every bite, any amount or kind of food. Trista and I never discussed what happened and now I wonder if she ever knew about any of this. Another gift from God, another challenge overcome and another dire need met at the perfect time.

I remember a friend once told me that God's timing is perfect. God doesn't give grace until we need it. I guess God was teaching both Trista and me about this. Sometimes I'm a slow learner. I prayed for God to never give up on me.

CHAPTER 19

§

Days at the hospital turned into weeks that were broken up by the weekend visits with Steph and Stephan. Time passed quickly when we were together but it was getting more difficult to entertain and fill the time in Trista's days. I remember the mini-series, *The Thornbirds*, starring Richard Chamberlain, was being featured on television and although Trista couldn't see it, she got caught up in it as I continued to share what was going on in the scenes and interactions between the characters. Actually it was pretty steamy content for her age but we enjoyed talking about the story plot together, woman-to-woman.

After *The Thornbirds* series ended, we were back to "what's next" to fill our day. We prayed, sang, said our Rosary and sometimes Trista asked me to read to her. There was a fairly good selection of books in the children's playroom at the hospital that we could check out and keep for extended periods. But all our normal means to fill the days were getting pretty old and Trista's recovery seemed longer this time than it had been after the first surgery.

One day Trista, out of sheer boredom, said that she couldn't take one more song sung, one more story read to her or one more television show with me translating the action. Totally out of ideas myself, I asked her what we should do. Her solution to our hospital boredom dilemma was so simple that I couldn't believe that it never entered my mind before now. Trista said, "Do what you do, Mom. You cut hair. There has to be some moms waiting around here with sick children just like you who would really appreciate a haircut or a new hairdo." Trista's plan also included the nurses getting me some cutting shears and spreading the word to the parents about what we were offering. Trista said that I would be taking her with me in her wheelchair so she could talk to the sick kids about not being afraid. We'd be a team, and we were.

Each day when we woke up we got excited to find out who we'd be visiting that day and it did seem so perfect to use this time to help other moms. But one day our nurse asked if I would cut the hair of a young male cancer patient, to which I said, "Sure!"

As I wheeled Trista into the young man's room, she, in her typical precocious way, just went ahead to get rid of the elephant in the room before I got started. "What's wrong with you?" Trista asked. He explained to her that he had leukemia and needed a haircut because he was getting married in a few days right there in the hospital. After sharing that he was a writer, he went on to explain that he wanted to surprise his fiancée with his new look. As I began cutting his hair he broke out into a terrible sweat that was worse than any woman I'd ever seen going through the most drenching hot flash. Because this was very embarrassing for him, the young man kept apologizing but I just kept on trimming hair. He loved his new hairstyle and was very grateful. Actually Trista and I were most grateful. We were helping other people instead of sitting in boredom. What a precious gift to be able to give back. We thanked God for this encounter as we ended our day back in Trista's room.

We never heard any more about this young man whose hair I cut that day or anything about the wedding that was scheduled to take place in several days. All we knew was that he was happy the day we were with him. It was a beautiful moment that we could talk about with Steph and Stephan when they came to visit us the next weekend.

After further discussion, I found out that not only did Trista have plans for me to cut hair but also plans to address the horrible music problem she and Stephan had experienced in the children's playroom. Her solution: to ask her dad to bring his guitar and sing to entertain the kids. Since my husband often played his guitar and sang for the children's Mass on Friday mornings at our church in Kentucky, this seemed like a perfect idea. So, we called Steph and made sure his guitar would be with him on the next weekend visit. Then Trista asked the director of the playroom if it would be all right for her dad to share some music with the children on Sunday afternoon. It all happened just as Trista had envisioned. We were grateful for the gift of great music and another opportunity to contribute something of value for the other children in the hospital.

CHAPTER 20

§

As Trista's vision continued to worsen, it seemed that her other senses were certainly heightened. Or maybe by spending so much time together she didn't need to see my face anymore to be able to read what was going on with me. Trista could now read my voice, even my silence. For no apparent reason at all, she asked me if I ever cry about what's going on with her and the family. I said that I did. She then asked me when and where I cried. *Such questions,* I thought.

I explained that I typically cried each night while I was in the shower and the tears would fall down with the water. After laughing about that she got very serious and asked if we could please cry together from now on. We did, right then—for a long time. I shut her hospital room door and we continued to cry more.

I remembered when I was a little girl and used to go to my dad crying about anything. I'd be very upset and dad always told me to keep crying, not to stop, because it was good for me. He said that it would clean my eyes out and I would feel better. *Such wisdom in that,* I was thinking. This is one of those moments for Trista and me. It was much better to be able to cry together and we both felt much better, without ever discussing or saying a word, once we were all cried out that day.

§

CHAPTER 21

SUMMER WAS COMING TO AN end and it was almost time for the school year to begin for Stephan. He was incredibly tall for his age and his feet had really taken a growth spurt over the long recess. At age 11 his growth hormones seemed to be in overdrive. While pondering his back- to-school needs one day it seemed that most of his clothes still fit reasonably well but he had clearly outgrown those tennis shoes. Michael Jordan tennis shoes were all the rage and Stephan wanted a pair badly. With our financial situation, I couldn't imagine us purchasing such a pricey shoe and I told him so. For the shoes Stephan wanted, I figured they would cost at least $30, which was way more money than we had to spend. Although trendy tennis shoes were not exactly my priority, I know that Trista had no problem putting this on her prayer list. She prayed about everything. Being a practical mom, I believed that the most important point about getting new shoes for our son was that they would fit his growing feet. All fancy expensive shoes would need to be on hold. So I decided that when Steph and Stephan came to visit on the upcoming weekend, we would decide what shoes would fit our budget and Stephan's needs.

One morning a couple of days later, Trista and I had a wonderful surprise. We had just gotten back to her room from the playroom when a nurse said there was a priest looking for us. Soon we saw our pastor, Fr. Delma, pop his smiling face in our doorway. We greeted him with hugs and were so excited that he drove all that way to see us. After updating us about all the latest church news and

Trista providing an update about what she had been up to, he said he needed to head back to Kentucky. He prayed with us and started to leave. While walking out of Trista's hospital room door, Fr. Delma motioned for me to join him in the hall a minute. He reached into his pocket and pulled out a $100 bill placing it into my hand. He said it was from someone who wished to remain anonymous, who thought we might need some back-to-school items for young Stephan. Being proud and embarrassed, my ego took over and I gave the bill back to him explaining that I couldn't accept it but thank you. Fr. Delma then quietly said as he looked me straight in the eyes: "It's a grace to give and a grace to receive. Let this person receive grace by sharing with you. You accept with grace, this gift that's being provided." Of course, I took the money and felt ashamed that my pride got in the way of God's provision through His people.

Stephan got his Michael Jordan tennis shoes to start the new school year as well as several other clothing items. I realized that God can do anything to supply our wants and needs whenever He wants to. For our son, it sure seemed like a need, and God was indeed generous to provide it.

§

CHAPTER 22

As I MENTIONED EARLIER, TRISTA had developed quite a crush on her young resident neurosurgeon, Dr. Rigsby. Well, that infatuation never waned. In fact, he began giving Trista an occasional hug when he visited her room. She was on cloud nine. I asked Trista what she thought he looked like since her vision was so poor. All she said was that he looked handsome to her. Dr. Rigsby's kindness to Trista was beyond anything we had ever experienced. Sometimes he'd come to her room, sit on her bed and just talk with her a while after he had finished his shift. What he did for Trista was totally out of the ballpark for a physician. He made her feel special and she looked forward to seeing him whenever he showed up.

One evening Dr. Rigsby came to visit Trista and asked if she and I would like to leave the hospital for an evening to attend a charity fundraiser for children's cancer research. Dr. Rigsby and several other doctors from Vanderbilt had formed a rock group, for which Trista's favorite resident was the drummer. This band was to be the featured entertainment at the facility near the hospital. Dr. Rigsby had arranged for two nurses to go with us in case Trista had any challenges. We could actually wheel Trista in her wheelchair because the venue for the event was so near the hospital.

Trista was so excited that we prepped her for several hours. She would barely eat. She had me put lipstick and mascara on her plus we must have gone through her very limited clothing wardrobe a dozen times. Because she had no hair she wore a small hat that covered most of her baldness. With the finishing touch—a mist of perfume—she was ready for her very first rock concert thanks to her resident neurosurgeon.

We arrived safely at the facility without incident and I was shocked to see that the place was absolutely packed with people, mostly from the hospital. Just like at a real rock concert, the lights were turned down low and the noise level was high. Trista loved the environment immediately. I took note of every expression of delight on her face while she was taking all of this in. At 13 this must have seemed like a dream.

Shortly after we were seated, one of the band members took command of the microphone and thanked everyone for coming and for donating to children's cancer research. All food and drink purchase proceeds would be going to the charity, too. I was as excited as Trista was! This looked like a pretty big deal and very professional compared to what I had previously experienced. All the doctors in the band wore scrubs and sounded fantastic up there as they played top hits one after another for about 45 minutes.

Then, without any introduction about what was going to happen next, the lights dimmed even more and a sole spotlight was on the drummer, Dr. Rigsby. In the deafening hush in the room, Dr. Rigsby softly announced, "This next song is for a very special lady, Trista France, who is sitting in the audience tonight. Trista, this song is for you from me." Tears welled up in Trista's eyes and I think she would have never forgiven anyone who would have made a sound during Dr. Rigsby's solo of the song *Desperado*. He had a beautiful voice. Who would have guessed that a surgeon would be a great singer?

After the song *Desperado* was over, I cried as I looked at how happy Trista was at that moment. What an evening for her, for us. What a gift that this young man was Trista's doctor. Thank you again, Lord. You have blessed us beyond our wildest dreams tonight.

§

CHAPTER 23

It was difficult to imagine that anything could ever top Dr. Rigsby's rendition of *Desperado*. Trista talked about it with everyone and I mean everyone! Trista even relived her experience in detail with a newly ordained priest who started coming to visit us from a nearby Catholic Church. So young and green was this priest that I know he spent a distorted amount of time with Trista because she was very open to talk about everything and never minded sharing her very candid opinions about any topic. Her personality seemed to really delight this young clergyman. Trista was authentic and told it exactly like she saw it, holding nothing back--which was a lesson for me, even today.

When the young priest came to visit, he often brought cassette tapes and a player because he loved music as did Trista. On one occasion he brought the music for *Joseph and the Amazing Technicolor Dreamcoat*, a new musical he had just seen starring Donny Osmond. Although Trista wasn't all that familiar with the Old Testament scripture context for this music, the priest got her up to speed so that the songs had meaning for her, too. It was a perfect way to learn and to pass the time for us.

When Steph and Stephan came on one particular weekend, we were given permission to check Trista out of the hospital just long enough for our family to attend Mass where the new young priest was associate pastor. It had been such a long time and it was a great gift for us all.

Our new friend, the young priest, came now at least once a week to see Trista and we looked forward to his visits although, as Trista shared, he was certainly no competition for Dr. Rigsby.

On one of these visits I was in the process of writing a *Body of Christ* talk I was scheduled to present on a Walk to Emmaus women's retreat weekend. This retreat is the ecumenical version of the Catholic Cursillo that Steph and I had attended not long after I came into the Church. Trista, gaining strength and mobility, was scheduled to be released from the hospital to begin a series of radiation treatments at Vanderbilt. This was preceded by a much needed long weekend at home. During this long weekend, if Trista was well enough and all went as planned, she and I would go to the Presbyterian Church and I would give this talk as a segment of the retreat being conducted at that time.

After spending countless hours writing this *Body of Christ* talk, I could hardly wait for our young priest-friend to read it and give me some feedback. He shared that he had also attended a Catholic Cursillo retreat weekend and was familiar with what the retreat team would be looking for from me to share with this group of about 80 women.

After intently reading what I had written, our priest-friend lifted his head and in complete honesty suggested that I throw my *Body of Christ* talk into the wastebasket and start over. This time, he strongly suggested, "Ask the Holy Spirit to help you write the talk." It seems that the talk I had shared with him was riddled with mindless platitudes and scripture references that sounded preachy instead of providing the witness about how God works through His people to provide the needs of all. At first horrified by our friend's response, I was soon grateful. I did as he suggested and threw the talk into the trash to which Trista laughed out loud.

I didn't write the new version of the talk that day or even the next day, but Trista and I continued to pray about it until one morning I could hardly contain myself to write fast enough as the words just seemed to pour out of me onto the pages. There was little effort on my part to come up with anything particular so I knew it was right and real and Holy-Spirit inspired. After reading it to Trista we agreed on the message and cried together because this talk served as a snapshot of the many ways God's holy people, His Church, had helped us. People of all faiths and lifestyles had come to our aid just as we needed whatever they provided. Although this talk exceeded the allotted timeframe the retreat leader had given me, it seemed to flow perfectly and to accomplish the objectives of this segment. So I was hesitant to change the talk merely for the sake of a decrease in time. The key message that we hoped retreat attendees would walk away with was that *we* are the Church and God wants each of us to simply make ourselves available to Him--whether we are a nurse, a housewife with a family, a dad sitting outside of a surgical waiting room or a cancer patient and her mom sitting in a hospital for a prolonged amount of time. Wherever we find ourselves is where God will use us. We are not all called to be missionaries in Africa but we can be grateful that those who are called to do that work make themselves available to God in that way.

Trista and I did make it home to Kentucky for that long weekend, prior to starting the series of 30 radiation treatments. She sat in her wheelchair in the Madisonville Presbyterian Church kitchen listening to me give this talk through the Emmaus Retreat loud speakers that were mounted on the walls.

Reflecting on that day, I now believe that the experience of writing and sharing our story was even more for our benefit than for the retreat attendees. It made me realize how powerful God is and that He is totally able to meet the needs of us all, even the needs we don't know we need. Scripture says, "Jesus is all in all." This is a powerful reflection for me.

CHAPTER 24

§

THE LONG WEEKEND HOME SURE didn't seem that long for our family and Trista and I were now back at Vanderbilt Hospital. We were renewed and energized by the Walk to Emmaus retreat, by our church family at Mass and by being in our own beds! It was excellent preparation for the next phase of Trista's treatment—radiation—to which we had no prior experience and had no clue what to expect.

Back in a regular hospital room, we were anticipating some physical freedom because Trista had most certainly become stronger and more mobile. We were told that each of the 30 radiation treatments wouldn't take more than an hour of time. What we were not counting on was the nurse telling us that Trista would be released from the hospital to come and go for the treatment. The fact was that we had absolutely nowhere to go! There was no money for a hotel room and most certainly not for a six-week stay.

Not wanting Trista to be concerned about our situation, I privately began to ask God what He wanted us to do. Trista had to have these treatments at Vanderbilt. I checked on that. Trista could sense my frustration without me saying a word and she suggested that we pray about it together. It was like she was the adult and I was the child. I remember thinking, why should we assume that just because someone is older that the person is more spiritually mature than a younger person. That was thought provoking!

The next day I wheeled Trista to the radiology department so that those doctors could map out, by literally drawing on Trista's head with a pen, to identify the precise spot that would receive the intensity of the treatment. After these doctors explained what the treatment would include and the potential side effects, we settled back into her hospital room still wondering where we would be sleeping once released from the hospital. I could not imagine that as nice as they all had been, that the nurses would put us out with nowhere to go. But they clearly explained that we couldn't stay there.

By the afternoon of that day, I began to gather our few belongings in preparation to leave to go where I had no clue. After lunch we tried to entertain ourselves with silly girl talk. But the uneasy, underlying current of waiting for God to provide for our need, when we were down to the wire, was grueling.

Into our room walked our friend, Allison. After sharing what she had been up to with the Life Flight Team, she said she heard we were being released from the hospital to begin radiation treatments. Allison explained that Dr. Rigsby's girlfriend was also a nurse and was Allison's apartment roommate. I was confused and reeling, trying to sort out all these connections in my mind. Allison soon made clear the reason for her visit to our room. Allison's roommate, Mitzie, would not need the second bedroom of their apartment for a while. Allison wondered if Trista and I would like to stay at her place for the six weeks of Trista's radiation treatments. Before I could even respond, Trista blurted out, "Sure!"

Believe it or not, that's how God provided for our need, just in time, once again. Unbelievable! It's like God set this whole thing up years ago. What a God we serve! What a loving God He is, working so often through his loving, generous people!

These accommodations would be perfect and because Allison's apartment was so close to the hospital, it was also incredibly convenient. Steph decided to leave a car with me so I could get Trista to her daily treatments and could easily drive home on the weekends.

CHAPTER 25

§

MOVING INTO ALLISON'S APARTMENT WAS a breeze since we had so few belongings to transport. Maybe there is a lesson there. If I don't have much, I don't have much to move. Hmmmm.

That first night sleeping together in Mitzie's big bed was more restful than I could have imagined. I didn't realize how accustomed I had become to all the activity at night in the hospital. Quiet was pure bliss. We slept in so late that Allison had already gone to work by the time we got up. It was the note that Allison left us on the kitchen counter that Trista and I both found such an amusing way to start our day once we shook off our grogginess.

It went something like this: "Grab whatever you want to eat. Oh, by the way, it seems we have a mouse. See you later, Allison."

Trista's eyes got big and the first thing she said was, "Where do you think it is, Mom?" Explaining that I had no clue, I began to look for signs of a mouse in the kitchen. It didn't take long for me to realize that the little critter had helped himself to the bread on the counter. The plastic bag surrounding the loaf had a decent-sized hole in it. It was plain to see that the mouse already had his meal and would likely be back for another tonight if we left the bread in the same spot.

As crazy as this sounds, that mouse was pure entertainment for us. Trista and I talked about him all the time. Trista would tip-toe across the living-room floor pretending that she didn't want to be surprised by stepping on the mouse. Interestingly, her vision was so impaired by this time that she couldn't have seen Mickey even if he had been lounging on her dinner plate. We laughed about this mouse every single day because he continued to elude Allison's daily traps. Then one day was his last. I can't say that I was sad that he went to be with the Lord, but he sure made our days in that apartment exciting.

Thinking about this mouse made me wonder if God had provided him to meet a need of ours. How long and boring those days would have been without him. I thanked God for this mouse and then I remembered one of my favorite stories written by Corrie Ten Boom in her book called *The Hiding Place* that was all about this concept but within a far graver context.

Corrie and her family owned a clock-making store in Holland. During World War II her family hid Jews from the Germans. The family was arrested for this crime, which resulted in her family being interred at a concentration camp. Separated from their parents, Corrie and her sister shared a huge dorm room with many other female prisoners. Conditions, as you can imagine, were deplorable. Beds were stacked high, one on top of another, with very little headroom to even sit up. The prisoners were packed into the makeshift dorm like sardines.

One day, Corrie tells of how this dormitory had become completely infested with fleas. Many of the women were repeatedly getting bitten by the fleas. Conditions were becoming even more unbearable for them all. Corrie and her sister recommended that all the women thank God for the fleas—the very ones that were eating them alive each day and night. Of course, the other women in the dorm believed that Corrie had lost her mind. But Corrie believed that everything was a gift from God, whether we like the gift or not. God's provision is what is best for us even when we don't recognize it as such. Although Corrie and her sister did lead prayer in that dorm and often talked to the other women about faith in Jesus, this must have been a pretty tough prayer to sell. But they did pray, thanking God for the fleas.

As the war progressed, many dormitories of women and men were led to their deaths by gas, as we have all read about in history publications. As it turned out, this particular dormitory of women that housed Corrie and her sister was never sent to execution because, as the women learned later, the German soldiers did not want to get this flea infestation onto themselves. Lives were actually spared because of these fleas!

God is in control; I'm convinced of that! No matter the circumstances in which we find ourselves, God has all means at His disposal to care for His people. It could even be fleas or a mouse. His love and care for each of us is greater than we can understand. Knowing that and labeling each moment as a holy gift from God, is pure peace.

In one of my favorite books, *The Joy of Full Surrender*, the author, Jean Pierre de Cassaude, puts it like this: "Passive faithfulness consists in the loving acceptance of all that God sends us each moment." This author suggests that continued acceptance is God working in us to make us holy. It is very simple. So simple that it takes grace for me to fully comprehend what this means in my life and to be able to apply it.

CHAPTER 26

§

THE WEEKS LIVING AT ALLISON's apartment quickly turned into a month. Because we now had a routine down that included the daily radiation treatments for five days, then a weekend home, it was all really all right. In fact, Trista seemed to show some signs of improvement although I sometimes wondered if I imagined that because I so desperately wanted my prayers for her healing to be answered.

After about the fifth week and 20 of the 30 prescribed treatments, Trista and I were headed home to spend the weekend with Steph and Stephan as usual. We were both looking forward to being home knowing that the ladies from my Prayer and Share Group would have the house spotless and there would be plenty of home-cooked food waiting for us.

This particular Friday we got on the road a little later than usual to begin our two-hour trip home for the weekend. Because rain was in the forecast, it was already starting to get dark outside and the clouds were making the sky look dark blue and in some places black. Trista was always more comfortable laying down on the back seat and typically would nap all the way home. The radiation treatments usually made her tired and she had just finished a treatment before we got into the car to head home. But this Friday was different and I knew it as the rain suddenly became torrential. It was like giant buckets of water were being tipped over from the sky to land just on our windshield. Traffic, now bumper to bumper, was presenting a scary driving scenario. But I decided that keeping up with the speed of the other drivers was best to get us home quickly through this horrible storm.

My decision to attempt to keep up with the flow of traffic turned out to be a bad one. By now I could barely see in between windshield wiper swipes and my concern about hitting the car directly in front of me grew. I remember trying to lean forward in my seat hoping to get a clearer view of the road but that didn't improve my vision at all.

Hearing the rain beat loudly against the car and feeling physically shaken by the thunder, Trista woke up and asked what was going on. I explained while trying not to upset her or make her afraid. She became upset anyway, but not because of the rain. She began to cry as she explained to me that she was in excruciating pain and couldn't stand it for very long. Since we hadn't expected this to happen, we had no medications or means to help her while we were in the car on the way home. Because this was before we had cell phones, I couldn't even call anyone to ask what to do.

I projected that we were about three-fourths of the way to Madisonville. That meant that we were about thirty minutes away from home, in the middle of nowhere, with a continuous downpour that didn't let up for a minute and my child was in the back seat now yelling in terrible pain. I had no idea what to do, so with tears filling my eyes I called out to God in great frustration and anger. Beating on the steering wheel, I told God that we couldn't take any more and pleaded with Him to relieve Trista of this pain. By this time I was all-out crying but Trista couldn't see me. She was writhing in the back seat trying to move around and somehow manage the terrible pain inside of her head.

The only solution that came to me was to exceed the speed limit, because where we were on the road now, there were no more cars. I would get to the Madisonville Hospital as quickly as possible, I decided. Out of the blue, Trista said, "Mom, tell me a story like you used to when I was little and were putting me to bed. It may get my mind off of the pain in my head so I can relax." At this point I was willing to try anything and so I began telling Trista a silly bedtime story I had made up for her and Stephan called, *Icky Bod*. I wasn't far into this tale when I noticed that Trista wasn't moaning anymore and within minutes she was sound asleep. At almost that exact same time, the rain totally stopped and I realized we were just minutes from home.

So I have to consider, was the *Icky Bod* story to calm me or Trista? Probably both of us. There wasn't a need for Trista to go to the hospital after all. Whatever had caused her intense pain had moved on and she felt good again. We were glad to be home.

While reading *My Utmost for His Highest* by Oswald Chambers, which has been one of my favorite daily devotional resources for many years, I read the following entry for August 11: "When you get to your wits' end and feel inclined to succumb to panic, don't; stand true to God and He will bring His truth out in a way that will make your life a sacrament."

No telling how many times over the years I read the message for August 11th, but now these words came alive for me. God had allowed me the gift to live them. If I had discounted Trista's solution to our dire situation in the car, I would have missed the blessing God had for us. Anyone can have the best idea, I decided, because if it comes from the Lord, it doesn't need to make sense to me. I just need to do it.

CHAPTER 27

§

ABOUT FIVE-AND-A-HALF WEEKS OF RADIATION treatments had been completed, with us staying with Allison in her apartment. Because Trista and I knew we would be going home for good very soon, we could hardly contain our excitement, nor could Steph and Stephan. We had become quite a team--with me, Trista and Allison. Plus we had made many friends at Vanderbilt Hospital. But as Dorothy said in *The Wizard of Oz*, "There's no place like home!" We were so ready to be a family again and Trista was feeling great. Praise God!

Word spread that Trista and I would be arriving home soon and it seemed like a party when we saw who was waiting for us there. Because Fr. Delma had kept our church family abreast of our circumstances and Trista's successful completion of the radiation treatments, people had brought over tons of food and the house was spotless. Our family was so incredibly grateful for it all.

In fact, we were only home a few days when I heard a knock at our front door. I peeked out the window and saw that there was a big delivery truck in our driveway. I remember thinking that there must be some confusion because ours was definitely the wrong house. After slightly opening the front door to tell the deliveryman that we weren't expecting anything, he explained that he was there to deliver a 60-inch-screen television. I argued with him until he finally showed me the delivery order that clearly showed our name and address. He then said, "An anonymous donor heard that your daughter could only see large images and this person bought a big television for her." The deliveryman then read directly from his chart, "Please tell the France family that if there comes a time when they no longer need this television, it is to be donated to Christ the King Catholic School." So, in came the big television and Trista was delighted, with her very impaired vision, to try and watch the musical *Annie*. What a beautifully practical gift!

CHAPTER 28

§

GETTING INTO A BIT OF a routine back at home, we also got back to attending weekly Mass at Christ the King church. It was a treasure to be with our church family who kept us in their prayers and cared for us the entire time Trista and I were in Nashville.

One of the many Christ the King parishioners we cherished was Louise Smith who was someone I had attended prayer meetings with before Trista got sick. Louise, who lived a very modest life in a small town on the outskirts of Madisonville, was blind but she hadn't always been blind. I had heard that Ezra, Louise's husband, had a drinking problem and sometimes became belligerent with both Louise and their son. As it was told to me, on one of those occasions when Ezra wasn't quite himself, he pulled out a gun in an effort to scare their son. Louise, stepping in between her husband and her son to protect him, was hit by a bullet from Ezra's gun that ultimately resulted in Louise's loss of vision.

Louise, a very godly woman and never one to complain, was only put out by her blindness when she became challenged to find their outhouse, especially during the winter months when there was snow on the ground. I also heard that sometime later, friends helped her out with the installation of her first indoor commode. I loved Louise Smith. She spoke very fast as though she was always in a hurry. She didn't stammer but rather was succinct about what she wanted to say. I can still see her with her shortly cropped snow-white, tightly permed hair, sunglasses, and short, rather stocky build. She was beautiful to me because I knew she loved Jesus more than anyone or anything. Louise, a fervent prayer warrior, prayed in ways I didn't fully understand but I knew she trusted Jesus for everything.

Louise decided that our entire salon staff, even though she didn't personally know them all, needed a "Daily Vitamin," as she called it, from the Lord. She asked for the names of every person who worked at The Village Salon so that she could pray for each one. The Lord would then give Louise a specific scripture verse for each person. At first I don't believe every person took this seriously, but they soon did. Each Friday morning when the salon had been open only a short while, someone from the staff would always ask who was going to call Louise to get our vitamins from the Lord! For this reason, we kept a Bible in the dispensary that was referenced, at a minimum, every Friday morning.

It was because of my great admiration for Louise that I agreed to accept her offer to teach Trista Braille, although Trista was not all that receptive to the idea.

Even though Louise had learned Braille as an adult and read it easily, she was a bit insistent that Trista, her very first pupil, learn it quickly--which simply didn't happen. After several lessons, Trista asked if she could not learn Braille from Louise anymore but did agree that she might need to learn it from someone at some time. Trista was getting bored and was ready to go back to school, to be in the eighth grade with her friends.

CHAPTER 29

§

IF TRISTA FELT WELL ENOUGH to go to school to be among her former classmates, although blind, with no hair and challenged to walk, we agreed to support her on this next adventure. What courage she has, I remembered thinking. Would I have been this brave? At the time when teenagers were about to enter high school, they were usually all caught up in appearances, group dating and attending school functions. Trista was ready to jump in with no self-consciousness about her disabilities at all. She believed she could do anything. She knew she was smart and she had maintained a small network of beautiful girlfriends her age who had supported her all along the journey of her illness. Getting back to school for Trista, and to us, was a healthy outward sign that we were finally making progress moving forward in our lives, putting all this illness business behind us and getting our "real" lives back.

We met with Trista's school principal who agreed that, by law, Trista was entitled to attend school as long as she could keep up with her course work and was mobile enough to get to class. Trista agreed with me that the course work would be the easier of the two qualifications since all of her teachers had agreed to provide her oral exams. The mobility issue, especially up and down stairways when changing classes, would require further strategy.

Holly, Trista's very best friend who lived down our street, as well as another classmate, offered quickly to help guide Trista to her classrooms and then get to their own. The plan seemed reasonable so it was now a matter of seeing how it would all work.

It was the first day back at school and Trista gave me strict orders not to walk into the school with her. She explained that her friends had it handled. I was instructed to pick her up at the end of the school day.

I remember watching as Trista, with her hat covering her bald head and her school books carried by her one working arm, marched proudly in through the front doors. Although she couldn't see, she knew that I must be watching her because she turned her body 180 degrees, just before stepping her foot onto the wood floor as if to say, "It's okay, Mom. Please let go for a little while. I need to do this on my own." She smiled and my heart sank inside, not because of her physical impairments but rather because I wasn't sure how the teachers or students would respond to her. Madisonville, Kentucky is a very small town. Numerous newspaper articles had been published about our family's situation regarding her illness and many churches of all faiths had lifted our needs to God in prayer. These kids and teachers knew about Trista even if they hadn't personally met her. Would her classmates treat her the same, ignore her, make fun of her? I just didn't know what to expect. However, she wasn't afraid at all—not one bit.

I asked God to protect Trista, to protect her courage, her strength and to give her a great "first day back-at-school experience" that would help her feel as though she fit in and not feel like an outcast. When we were at Vanderbilt the environment was a completely level playing field because every child there was ill, dealing with day-to-day challenges presented by their maladies. In this school environment, Trista was suddenly not like the other kids, and I wondered if these physical differences would make even her closest classmates uncomfortable. Is it "cool" to socialize with a bald, blind, limping teenager? It broke my heart for her but I realized that Trista had always spoken her mind, been her own person with no indication of self-consciousness ever. She couldn't have cared less about being in the "in" crowd before she got sick, although she always wanted her hair to look stylish and she had always taken great pride in getting all A's in school. I just had to trust God to take care of her as we had done numerous times before today. This situation, although not life-threatening, had capacity to also change Trista forever.

When it came time to pick Trista up after her first day, I was in the car as I spied her walking out of the building laughing with her two girlfriends. Since the plan was that I take the friends home, it was quite an entertaining recap of the day's events from each of them.

The girls shared that it wasn't an easy day. In fact, on one occasion Trista fell on the stairs as her books flew out of her hand. Everyone helped, the girls recounted, even kids they didn't know. Teachers all welcomed Trista into their classrooms. Trista, with great excitement in her voice and energy in her body language, couldn't wait to share with me all the things she learned this day. *Praise God!* I thought. *Thank you, Lord,* I said to myself. *Thank you for these two beautiful friends and especially for the big smile on Trista's face. Thank you!*

After several days of school had successfully gone by, I toyed with the thought of going to our salon and possibly doing some client's hair for the first time in many months. Lord knew we needed the money. So, I boldly stepped back into the doorway of our business and made a few phone calls to discover that some of my former customers were up for new hairdos on both Thursday and Friday as a start. I decided to work only during Trista's and Stephan's school hours.

On Friday, one of my clients was Velma Davis, a woman from our church who had attended the Catholic Cursillo retreat when I had attended. She was also at my group's table of St. Cecelia, the group of women who each had a grief story to share. Velma was also a member of our Prayer and Share Group. I typically shied away from much one-on-one conversation with Velma since Trista and I had gotten back. Not because she wasn't a kind person but because she lost her young son to cancer. As a Mom, I didn't want to hear about her son's death in any context. I felt so sorry for her loss but such talk frightened me now. Trista was doing well, was back in school. Our family was moving forward.

What Velma shared with me that day while I was styling her hair haunted my thoughts. She said she totally understood that I was trying to financially support our family, but if there came a day when Trista needed to stay at home, she and her husband John would provide the equivalent money of my earnings so I could stay with her. This seemed odd that she would say this to me, like I would ever consider putting salon income as more important than being with my child. Not wanting to be rude, I thanked her and assured Velma that this would never be necessary.

Later that day, it struck me that Velma was trying to say something that had totally eluded me at the time. She, in her kindness, was trying to let me know, that from her experience of losing her child, she would not want me to take one minute away from being with Trista because she might not always be here. She wasn't suggesting that I would put money as a priority. Velma was telling me that the moments with Trista are precious and we don't have any idea how many are left. I felt terrible that I had misjudged Velma's intent and realized I should have thought better of her. I asked God to forgive me and I knew in my heart that I would never take her and John up on their offer. I also knew that I didn't care if we lost everything we had ever worked for if I could exchange it for Trista's healing or her life. I just had to trust God to take me down this path one day at a time. But Velma gave me tremendous pause for thought and prayer.

CHAPTER 30

§

IT WAS NOW TRISTA'S THIRD week back at school and I was working part-time in the salon when one day I got a call from Trista and Stephan's principal requesting a meeting with him. Feeling encouraged about Trista's progress and her teacher's on-going support, I was thrilled to accept his meeting request even though I had no idea what subject we would discuss.

As I got seated in the large chair across from the principal I was totally caught off guard, as Mr. Higgins informed me that Trista could no longer attend this school. It seems that some of the students and teachers were complaining to him that friends who were helping Trista get to her classes were often late for their own classes. Teachers were frequently having to wait to start class and the logistics required to help Trista were beginning to be too much work for the friends plus too inconvenient for the teachers. He explained that although Trista could legally attend this school, no one would be available to assist her to get to any class, or lunch, or enter and leave the building. Special considerations and concessions for Trista would end—starting immediately.

Keep in mind that Madisonville is a small town and our family had known this principal and his family ever since Trista and Stephan had started school eight years prior. I was angry, hurt and wondered how in the world I would explain this to Trista. Without the help of her friends, there simply was not any way that Trista could get to classes. My thoughts went to Trista's conversation with us about getting through eighth grade so she could start high school. She loved school, always got excited about learning and enjoyed being with her friends in the school environment.

After praying about how to tell Trista the news, I realized that I had to get myself in order to be in the right frame of mind. Maybe God was moving Trista along to be open to get the specialized help that she needed and the only way this could happen was for the traditional school channel to be closed. Once I got my head on straight, got over any animosity with Mr. Higgins, her dad and I explained the situation to Trista in a context we believed would be palatable for a thirteen-year-old. Unbelievably, Trista didn't get upset, angry or have much to say about it at all. Maybe she had been challenged getting around more than she had let us know. Had she been going to school for us because she thought we wanted it? Maybe going back to school, even with disabilities, was for us all to be able to get a taste of how it used to be before she got sick. But the truth was, Trista wasn't the same and neither were we. Isn't it funny how much importance we place on fitting in when God sends the circumstances to grow us up and showcase how unique He had made each of us? Our family talked through all of this and decided we were on our own unique path that had to include meeting our unique needs.

CHAPTER 31

§

SEVERAL DAYS HAD PASSED SINCE we gave Trista the news about not being able to attend her former school. Trista sat us down to share some news of her own with us. Trista explained that she needed to learn in a way that was right for her. So, she said, that meant she would need to check into attending a school for the blind. Not knowing what this would entail, we agreed to explore information about schools closest to us and to speak to representatives of the different available programs. One thing I did know was that I would *never* be okay with sending Trista off somewhere to go to school. A promise is a promise and I gave my word that I would never leave her.

What is that old saying about when we plan, God laughs? That said, the information we gathered led us to the closest school for the blind, which was about two-and-a-half hours from Madisonville in Louisville, Kentucky. Students boarded there and the program, at first exposure, seemed amazingly effective in teaching a young unsighted person not only the age-appropriate curriculum but also life-skills. Trista realized she now desperately needed all of this if she was going to thrive beyond our home and community.

So, it was time for a family field trip to check out this school although I had no intention of letting Trista live there away from us. Never! This trip was to placate Trista. I was certain they likely had external resources for families who chose not to board their children at the facility. In a way, I hoped it would be an awful place, giving Trista a poor first impression. Or, maybe we'd see that it was dreadfully dirty and teachers appeared unskilled or mean. Totally disappointed, Steph and I realized that it was none of the above. It looked much nicer than a college dorm room although much more organized and functional for unsighted children. Trista was so excited because being at this school once again leveled the playing field for her as it had been leveled at Vanderbilt. Her dad, Stephan, and I were the minorities in this environment.

The sounds, the smells, the tones of the staff's voices and other students were like vitamins giving an energy boost to Trista's emotional state. Because we often now knew exactly what was going on with Trista by her facial expressions, we could read what was going on inside of her pretty easily. There was absolutely no sign of fear or anxiety. For her, it was like a great adventure. As staff members explained what typically happened in each room when we toured the building, it seemed as though Trista could see herself in her own mind doing these things. She liked it there. That was obvious to us all.

What we didn't realize was that while taking the school tour, the staff was also checking Trista out to determine if she was a good candidate for this facility and its educators.

After the tour, we all sat in the office of the principal who explained that Trista would need to board at the school for the balance of the school year and then go home for the summer. Although I didn't say a word, Trista knew my position about this. Not wanting to be unfair, I shared with the principal that our family would go home, pray about it, talk to Trista's doctors and let them know our decision. The principal shared she was thrilled at the prospect of having Trista as a student because, she said, "Trista is happy, seems grounded and is eager to learn."

It was quiet on the drive home from the school because there was so much to think about. The silence was broken by Trista when she said, "Mom and Dad, if you love me, let me go to school there." Although her words dug deeply into my "mom state of mind," that wanted to keep her children close to home, to protect them and at the same time equip them with knowledge and skills to thrive in this world, I kept silent. Trista knew exactly how to cut to the chase with me; we had been through a lot together.

After another physical check-up, Trista had her doctor's permission to attend the Louisville School for the Blind. Her dad and I ultimately decided that we had to let her have this opportunity to learn in an environment that made sense to her. Her courage amazed me. I wondered, if in a similar situation, I would have been so brave. Nevertheless, I did know that to not let her try would be selfish. To my mind, Trista, having been through so much, had become a very mature 13-year-old who had earned the right to be given this opportunity, or any opportunity she needed to learn, to grow, and to function on her own.

Saying good-bye to Trista, as we three walked out of that dorm room, was one of the toughest moments in my life that I can remember. I knew that God would protect her. I also knew that at this time, this was the right place for her. But, like any mom, I was giving her up to independence, to entry into adulthood, to a place where she wouldn't need me. This was painful. I felt selfish and thought to myself, *"It's not about you. It's about Trista."* As rational as that thought was, I still cried and ached for her as if I had given up my baby to someone else's arms. Letting go is painful. Change is painful. Realizing that life isn't all about me and what I want is painful.

CHAPTER 32

§

OF COURSE, WE CALLED TRISTA every single day and she shared with us how learning Braille was tough. She said that the teachers were also tough but fair and weren't ever angry with the students. She liked her teachers and told us she was doing fine. Trista also shared exactly how many weeks it would be until the school session would be over and she would be home. Any college student would have likely given relatively the same sort of report, so we laughed about it and assured her that we would call the next day. It may have been difficult for Trista to get to the phone each day because she recommended that we wait until the following week to check in with her. We agreed to the day and time before ending our conversation with our typical closing words of, "I love you." and "Good-bye."

Sharing all the family updates on the phone with my mom several days later, Mom asked if we would like to take a few days away with her and Dad and go to Florida to stay at my uncle's guesthouse at Vero Beach. She envisioned that since it was only for a couple of days away, Dad would drive us down, we'd stay a few nights then come right back. Mom was pretty convincing that Steph and I needed a break while Trista was at the Louisville School for the Blind and we could ask one of Stephan's friends' parents if he could stay with them.

To this day I can't believe that we agreed to go. But the entire world knew our contact information and we agreed to call Trista's school and Stephan's friend's parents every day while gone. We truly enjoyed time spent away with my parents because they always laughed a lot, loved life, were always encouraging and made even the simplest things so much fun.

We four—Mom, Dad, Stephan and I-- made the quick trip south with no problems and the conversation in the car about my parents' eclectic group of friends and neighbors kept us roaring with laughter. Uncle Carl and Aunt Ruth were gracious hosts and recommended that we go to Disney World one afternoon since it was near our guesthouse. We did and it was great fun although the weather turned unseasonably cold and we all had to buy sweatshirts to keep warm as we walked around the park.

Once back at my uncle's guesthouse, we got an unexpected call from a representative of the Louisville School for the Blind, where Trista now resided. Trista's condition was quickly deteriorating. Her continuous headaches, as well as inability to walk, were making it impossible for her to attend class or get around at all. "We'll be right there as quickly as possible," I assured them.

Of course, my first thought was that the tumor may have grown back again. I didn't allow my mind to stay with that thought for very long. Maybe anxiety caused by being in a different environment coupled with so much change had been too much for her. We still felt as though we had made the best decision for Trista by letting her try.

When we got to the school to retrieve Trista, she was in great pain. We called her Madisonville doctor before leaving Louisville to ask what we should do. He recommended that we bring her directly to the Madisonville Hospital ER to be examined. We wasted no time getting her there.

After an MRI, it was evident that Trista's brain tumor had returned and we were told to head to Vanderbilt the next day for her to be checked in and to determine her next course of treatment. Before getting sick to my stomach, I thanked God for these few weeks He had given us and I recalled the many things our family had done together—watching her favorite shows on the large-screen television, going to Mass as a family, all four of us simply spending time in our home, her going to eighth grade with her classmates, learning while at the Louisville School for the Blind. These were all tremendous gifts that none of us took for granted.

§

CHAPTER 33

AGAIN, TO MY PUZZLEMENT, TRISTA didn't seem very upset about hearing this news. She seemed neither angry nor concerned but rather deep in thought and reflective. After we called Fr. Delma to share what was going on, he recommended that we stop at church before leaving for Vanderbilt so we could all pray together, and we did.

Because we were seasoned patients, checking into the hospital and settling into Trista's room was a painless process. Our friends, Allison, the floor nurses and parents of kids we knew from when we were there last, greeted us with smiles, yet were generous not to ask why we were back.

After much silence, Trista reflected again on all the things we had done since we left the hospital last time and was in story-telling mode about all her experiences with anyone who came into her room to visit. Since we weren't scheduled to see Dr. Meecham or Dr. Rigsby until the following morning, we settled down to sleep after asking God to help us rest.

But I couldn't sleep as I imagined every conceivable scenario about Trista's treatment options we might hear about from her doctors in the morning. I practiced what I would say in response. From, "Nothing we can do," to, "Time for another surgery." Or, "Let's do more radiation." And even, "Let's explain a new experimental process we might try." Although not certain, I suspected Trista had the same discussions going on in her head. She was unusually quiet for the rest of the night.

Morning came and in walked our two neurosurgeons with facial expressions like soldiers ready for battle. Although their faces were smiling, their words brought no smiles to our faces. Although they were kind and respectful, I wasn't glad to see them again. I had hoped our only future communication with them might be in the form of Christmas cards once a year. That wasn't to be. Their recommendation was to perform a third surgery to remove the new tumor. Trista said nothing. I responded that we would discuss it and be open to talk more about it later in the day.

Desperately trying to understand the magnitude of the seriousness surrounding this impending operation, I had an in-depth discussion about it with Allison and Trista's attending nurse. I asked the floor nurses if they would be willing to bring me some medical resources or literature about the type of tumor Trista had, an ependymoma, that had formerly been classified as an astrocytoma, so I could be more informed about what we were up against.

From the information I gathered, no child had ever survived an ependymoma to date and there was no known cure. Because Trista was now down to less than one hundred pounds and was five feet six inches tall, I considered how her withered, frail body could withstand another surgery. After acquiring relevant knowledge, to my limited degree of understanding, I became increasingly angry that the doctors had not explained to us what I now knew--the degree of severity we were facing with this cancer. In my anger I had a conversation with Dr. Meecham down the hall from Trista's room where she couldn't hear us. "Why didn't you tell us how bad this was and that no one has ever survived it? You led us to believe that Trista could get well, that you removed all the cancer in the surgeries." In all humility, Dr. Meecham explained that he never knows a definite prognosis and it is his job to offer options, perform his best treatment and hope that healing is the result. I was still angry, but maybe not as much with the doctor as I was with the cancer that kept coming back. I considered the potential difference in the quality of life that Trista could have had these past 15 months had he told us there was no hope. He said that no one can tell you with all certainty that there isn't any hope. He also explained that Trista would have the same risks during this surgery that were present in the two prior, only this time we should expect a more difficult and prolonged recovery process. Somberly looking me straight in the eyes, "There's no guarantee that the tumor won't grow back again," he said.

My anger somewhat now in check, I went back to Trista's room where she was patiently waiting to talk with me. She said these words as best I can remember. "Please Mom. I don't want another surgery. I'm tired and just want to go home. Can we please just go home?" It's as though she knew everything Dr. Meecham and I had discussed even though she couldn't have heard a word of it. I looked down at her frail body and again knew in my heart Trista had earned the right to make this decision. Nevertheless, I couldn't tell her what I was thinking.

After talking the situation over with Steph and praying about it at great length, we agreed we would bring Trista home after a permanent shunt was placed in her skull. This shunt would relieve pressure from the fluids that would cause her pain as the new tumor continued to grow inside her brain.

CHAPTER 34

§

IT WAS SO GOOD TO be home!

Stepping back into our former way of life and familiar environment was a precious gift. Again, the women from my Prayer and Share Group had the house spotless along with food ready to eat right out of the refrigerator and the freezer, too, this time. Mom decided to come down from Akron to stay with us and help me. Those beautiful sisters in Christ could then take a much-needed break from maintaining our household as well as their own each week.

How Trista loved being in her own room, her own bed, listening to her favorite music through her headset and "picking" on her brother again. You might have thought that this sister and brother, at this point, would have been super sweet to each other but that certainly wasn't the case. For this, I was grateful! To hear those two kids disagree and fuss at each other was a most loving thing to hear. Because these siblings always seemed to work it out, I didn't intervene. I could tell that they both enjoyed the bantering and they enjoyed making fun of me, and their dad, at every opportunity.

Trista and Stephan now spent hours recounting the many times growing up when they had delicious moments of humor at our expense. Like when we bought them a male and female guinea pig, named Fred and Ethel, after the characters on the Lucille Ball television show. Our intent was to teach our children the facts about reproduction, the real facts of life, so we could have the "big talk" with them using these two, cute, furry creatures as examples.

Well, it wasn't long before we noticed that Ethel was most certainly "with pig" and Steph and I nervously got through the topics of love, marriage, reproduction and how God did it all. We were relieved when the talk was over and were feeling pretty confident and proud that we had explained it thoroughly within the context of our Christian faith. Steph and I later discussed that by the look on the kids' faces, we had nailed it. Once we were done with the talk, our kids told us thanks and that they "got it."

Now, years later, as we sat on Trista's bed in her room, Stephan and Trista told us that they already knew all this information from family-living class at school. They let us know what they were really thinking that day while we were sweating through the "talk." Laughing so hard that tears were streaming down Stephan's face, he and Trista confirmed that our "talk" had made them laugh for weeks and that the verbiage we used in our explanations could take them to hysterics any time they needed a good laugh.

It was so good to laugh together that I could not have cared less about being the brunt of their humor. And so they went on sharing other whacky things we did that made them laugh when we weren't aware of it. Trista and Stephan, only 16 months apart in age, were real buddies. Friends who were as different as two siblings could be, but they loved each other deeply, shared dreams of their futures together. I pray they always knew how much we appreciated their uniqueness.

Because we were home and knew the new tumor was still growing, Dr. Brewer, Trista's Madisonville pediatrician, wanted us to understand what to expect with her illness as it progressed. I believe that Dr. Rigsby tried to explain these same things to me before we left Vanderbilt but I couldn't hear him at that time. All I could hear was that we were going home. So Dr. Brewer told us that as the tumor continued to grow, Trista could go into a coma, could be in terrible pain due to the increased pressure in her brain and that her body would eventually begin to shut down. What he said that day still hadn't sunk in. Right now, our family needed to celebrate being home together.

But Dr. Brewer wanted us to understand that Trista's prognosis wasn't positive. He also wanted us to know that he and his wife, Edie, were moving to Illinois soon. He was trying to prepare me for his move to Chicago and more importantly, for Trista's death.

These words didn't seem real to me although I could clearly see that Trista was getting worse. She had lost a lot of weight. At five feet six inches, she was now well below one hundred pounds. Because her stomach was often upset, she ate very little, causing her to be weak and unable to walk across the room without our help. Trista knew she was declining, yet we never spoke of it.

In fact, one day Trista shared the reason why her stomach hurt badly all the time. Because she hadn't had a period in about a year, she determined that this abrupt halt of natural flow would give any woman a stomachache. However, she knew there was more going on than her lack of menstruation.

Walking into her room with breakfast one morning, Trista caught me totally off guard when she point blank asked, "Mom, you promised you would always tell me the truth. Am I going to die?"

I remember trembling at the sound of her words and realizing this was a defining moment for Trista, for our relationship, for truth. I responded, "Trista, the doctors don't believe you will live but as you know, that's God's call."

As soon as the words left my mouth I felt sick inside and Trista began to cry loudly. She wailed, to the point that her dad walked into her room to ask what was going on. Once I told him, his look of horror and anger at me ripped my insides out. After several minutes of all of us crying and Trista's uncontrollable yelling finally stopped, Trista, in a completely calm demeanor told us that she had wanted to grow up, to finish school, but knew all along that she wouldn't survive the cancer. Trista explained that she was angry and upset that we now knew she would die. Her struggle was with the pain as well as the suffering this would cause all of our family.

What 13-year-old thinks like this? I thought. Her frustration and pain were not for herself but for us. Even though I had said the words out loud, nothing about them seemed real to me yet. I still believed that God could and would answer our prayers for healing, but I sure hoped He would hurry it up. Should I have lied to Trista, made everyone feel more comfortable so we could pretend a while longer that she wasn't getting worse? All I knew was that I had made Trista a promise to always tell her the truth. After all the suffering she had gone through to this point, I believed she deserved the truth from me.

Once the three of us were relatively calm again, there was a great feeling of relief that the biggest elephant in the room was finally gone. I wondered if some of our family and friends in the medical field already knew Trista's prognosis. Very thankfully, if they did know, they let our family get to the conclusion in our own way and in our own time.

Now what? I thought. For no reason I can think of, I felt like we would be all right. Maybe Trista got us to this point. There was no sadness and no complaints. There were friends and family ready to help us and they seemed to come from everywhere.

Dr. Brewer, Trista's pediatrician who first discovered the tumor, was a family friend, as was his wife Edie. I had been doing her hair at our salon. We all presumed that Dr. Brewer would be Trista's physician until he left for Illinois. We didn't realize that the move was going to be so soon. On a visit to our house one day, he explained we needed to find another doctor to take his place. This was so tough to hear because Dr. Brewer was incredibly kind to Trista and helpful beyond all normal doctor and patient relationships that I had experienced—except maybe for Dr. Rigsby, Trista's heart-throb neurosurgeon. What doctor makes his patient homemade bread he called "gut bread" and brings it to his patient along with fresh-picked strawberries?

Thinking Trista would be upset knowing that the Brewers were leaving, we were all surprised once again when Trista said it was no problem that Dr. Donley, an orthopedic surgeon who also attended

Christ the King Church, would be her new doctor. After I explained to Trista that Jim Donley, although very nice, was a bone surgeon, Trista explained that she still wanted only him to be her new doctor. As off the wall as this sounded to us, Jim Donley agreed!

Before the Brewer family actually left town for Chicago, I received a call from Edie Brewer who asked if she could come over for a talk. Always enjoying her company and forthright manner, I was actually excited to have her visit. When she began to speak I wasn't prepared to hear her topic. Edie explained that her mother had recently died and one of the most difficult aspects of losing her Mom was making the funeral arrangements by herself. Because of her recent experience, she wanted to know if she could help me with Trista's. Almost numb at the prospect, I agreed.

Edie helped me in a way no one else had thought about, and her timing was sensitive to our family and me. She explained that when we really love a family member who passes away, it is easy to get caught up in funeral arrangements that are truly not needed and, without realizing it, end up with a huge bill. Neither Steph nor I had any prior experience in making arrangements since no one close to us had ever died. How does one prepare to make these decisions before the death occurs? I trusted Edie who explained frankly that the day God takes Trista is not the ideal time to be selecting caskets or liners to go inside them.

The day came for Edie and me to meet at the funeral home. I was petrified to even walk through the door. My dad had a real fear of funeral homes in general and he passed that fear onto me. In addition, I had acquired a fear of my own from the only other funeral home experience I had had to date.

During earlier years of hairdressing in Kentucky, one of our regular salon clients had requested that I style her hair for her funeral one day. I didn't know anything about this request until her niece informed me once the woman passed. *How hard can this be?* I thought. The niece was always kind to me and I was glad to be able to show support for her family experiencing this difficult loss.

Wanting to be very professional, I gathered all my equipment, not knowing what was needed, and walked right into the funeral home office giving the impression that I had done this many times before.

The funeral home attendant led me upstairs where the elderly woman's body was lying on a slab, covered only by a sheet, her head propped up by what looked like a cement block. "What did the family want done today?" I asked, still attempting to appear confident. "A cut and style." the attendant replied. "Will you be staying here with me?" I asked. "No. I have work to do downstairs. I'll be back in a while to check on you. Oh, by the way, you do know that you only need to worry about styling the front of her hair and you can't use heat on her?" "Thanks," I replied.

The woman left the room and I made sure the door was left open. Going into self-preservation mode, I immediately decided to mentally remove myself from this situation by singing and, with a fierce resolve, to work as fast as possible to get out of there quickly.

After completing the trim, I thought I heard my friend Tara's voice and I was right. In a minute she was walking into the room. I was relieved to see her. She said she would stay until I was finished although what she was about to do almost made me sick. It seems that she got hungry before she came to the funeral home and had stopped at Long John Silver's. Her plan was to take a seat by the wall and eat her dinner in the room with me until I finished doing this woman's hair. As I looked out of the corner of my eye I glimpsed at Tara putting that big piece of fried-battered fish into her mouth. I looked back at the corpse whose hair I was styling. Again, I had to emotionally remove myself from the situation until I was done. I don't have any recollection of what the woman looked like but I can still see her body, her head on that block and her finished hairstyle which looked a lot like the picture her family had given me.

This incident was so scarring to my psyche and was a huge contribution to my negative impression of funeral homes that I couldn't ever again touch the scissors that touched that woman's hair. I committed to myself that that was the first and last time for me to ever put myself in that position.

After quickly reflecting on these fearful funeral home experiences, I decided Trista's body would not ever be viewed in the funeral home. She would only receive necessary required processes via the funeral home and then be taken to our church. The funeral home director agreed.

I was incredibly thankful for Edie that day. I didn't know about such things and she was kind enough to take the time to help me.

At this time there was another person who positioned herself to help us. It was Trista's piano teacher, Sandy Spera. Although we didn't know it, Sandy had been taking classes to become a qualified hospice volunteer, in case we would ever need her. Who does that? This thrilled Trista because she truly liked Sandy and looked forward to her frequent visits.

CHAPTER 35

§

YOU MAY HAVE THOUGHT THAT during this time life moved more slowly or that we could have gotten bored. The opposite is true; God just kept sending the people to help us at exactly the right time. God had it all planned out before we were born, according to scripture. I was beginning to get the picture about this.

A confirmation of that scripture passage was evidenced late one evening when Steph was working, Stephan was at a friend's house and Trista started feeling poorly. She tried to get up by herself and fell, breaking her toe. The pain was excruciating and I decided to take her to the hospital to get her seen by someone in case there was something they could do for her.

It wasn't easy getting her into the car but she and I devised a plan that worked. Once we got to the hospital, I realized I had to park a little distance from the door since it didn't seem right for us to enter through the ER doors. Trista was not in an emergency sort of condition this time. I thought I might need to take her through the ER door, though, because she couldn't walk and I couldn't carry her. Getting ready to pull out of the space where we were parked, a car pulled up right next to us. It was Fr. Glahn, our friend who was instrumental in getting us into the Catholic Church.

"What are you doing here?" I asked. "I saw your car on the highway and thought you might need some help when I realized you were pulling into the hospital," he answered. We hadn't seen Fr. Glahn since before Trista was diagnosed, but he knew all about her condition and offered to help us by carrying her into the hospital.

Trista appreciated the offer and laid her head on Fr. Glahn's shoulder as he gently lifted her from the car. As he was carrying her across the parking lot he said to Trista, "You've suffered a lot, haven't you, Trista?" "Yes Father, I have," she responded. "Always remember that Jesus suffered more," he said.

When Fr. Glahn said these words, a little anger rose inside me. After all, Trista was just a little girl and I wasn't sure she could grasp such profound thinking. But I was wrong. It was relevant and she had understood what Fr. Glahn meant. Because, from that day forward, whenever we said our Rosary together and we got to the Sorrowful Mystery about when Jesus was getting scourged at the pillar, Trista would cry. She would say, "How could we do this to our Lord?"

What I didn't realize the day Fr. Glahn carried Trista into the hospital was that he was also dying from cancer. He went to be with the Lord shortly after Trista left us.

God sent Fr. Glahn to us that day and because I know that our God is a frugal God, wasting no opportunity, this meeting in the parking lot benefitted them both. Only those who are dying could possibly know such truths to share. Both Trista and Fr. Glahn were living them out one day at a time.

But no one came more quickly to our aid than my mom. Determined to leave her home and Dad in Akron, she moved in with us to take over household responsibilities. She was an angel from heaven for us all. With Mom at the house, I could spend all my time with Trista and Stephan and with Steph when he wasn't working. Since no one could possibly know how long Mom would need to stay, Dad didn't come down until much later.

Dad had a very special relationship with Trista. I do think that seeing her so sick day after day would have been too tough on him. I think Trista was aware of this and was agreeable with his decision to stay in Akron. But Dad did write her letters and called frequently.

He had a special humor that only he and Trista shared. Whenever Trista was on the phone and I heard laughter I knew it was my dad talking to her.

If I could make a chart listing all the family members and friends who were helping us at this time, it would cover the entire kitchen table. In fact, there were many people we had never even met who did things for us. Someone—to this day we don't know who—set up a bank account for us so that people could deposit contributions anonymously. Our bills were being paid before they were even due and groceries and prepared food flowed through our house continually. I think Mom enjoyed the socialization she had through conversation with all these people. We were continually amazed at the kindness that kept coming and didn't wane for a single day.

Our salon receptionist, Betty Walker, and her husband, Don, came to the house to visit us one evening. Because of their deep and practical faith, I had learned by spending time with Betty how to have a more intimate relationship with Christ. Having prayed together about everything and anything over the years, we had given so many of our trials and praises to the Lord together. Betty was truly another of my genuine sisters in Christ who I loved dearly. On this particular occasion, the purpose of Betty and Don's visit was not to pray with us, as I had imagined, but rather for this beautiful couple to hand us a check made out with the sum total of their savings written on it. I knew this was a huge sacrificial gift and I also knew we couldn't accept this gracious gesture. After they left, I remembered wondering if I could be that generous.

§

CHAPTER 36

So NOW WE SEEMED SET up to get through each day with plenty of food, a reasonable routine for everyone. Our bills were getting paid on time and our new doctor was in place. Even the Louisville School for the Blind, wanting to ensure Trista had entertainment, sent books on record for her to enjoy. We were doing our best to stay positive, appreciate each day as a gift and trust God for everything.

One day while Trista was chilling out in her wheelchair still attempting to watch that big-screen television in the living room, Mom alerted us that Trista had a phone call. Not knowing who in the world was at the other end of this call, I kept whispering to Trista to tell me who it was. All I could see was that her eyes lit up and she grinned and handed me the phone.

Seems that a boy from her eighth-grade class was asking us if he could take Trista out to a drive-in on a date! He explained to me, and he clearly had this well planned out, that her dad and I could drive them. Trista and this boy would sit in the back seat for their date. What was most challenging about all this was that Trista was blind and this young man had a terrible stutter. So it took quite a while for him to get all of this articulated to me. My heart truly went out to him as I'm sure his stuttering was exacerbated by his nervousness in speaking to me about his "date idea." I told him that Trista's dad and I would need to discuss his request and that he could call us back later that evening for our answer.

Two months away from her fourteenth birthday, Trista had never entertained the thought that she would be asked out on a date or that we would ever allow her to go if she was asked. Chomping at the bit and in a constant giggle, Trista could barely contain herself until her dad walked through the front door, home from work.

Young Stephan thought the whole idea was ridiculous. He told us that he knew this boy and he definitely wouldn't be anyone Trista would be interested in dating. Keep in mind that Stephan was 11 years old! But Trista knew this boy, too, and she said he was really nice to her when she tried to go back to school. "He treats me normal," she explained. With Trista's ability to charm her dad into her way of thinking, it was a slam-dunk. Trista would be going on her first date in just two days—this coming Saturday.

I don't remember a lot about that Saturday evening, and I have no idea what movie the boy translated the action scenes to Trista about, but I've never forgotten how this young man made Trista feel. These two young people held hands and talked the entire evening, even with his difficult stuttering. Since they mostly whispered, we couldn't hear what they said but as the evening came to a close and we took him home, pulling into his driveway, he thanked Trista for going with him. He thanked her dad and me for taking them and he leaned back to give Trista a kiss good-bye right on her lips. I cried and so did Trista. It was a precious moment, a most loving and innocent moment and I thanked God for it again and again.

Still reeling from her "first ever" date, Trista got another phone call from someone in Nashville who wanted to know if he could stop by the house to visit her. You got it! It was Dr. Rigsby, her resident neurosurgeon from Vanderbilt Hospital in Nashville. We couldn't believe that this young man, his girlfriend Mitzie and our dear friend Allison, drove two hours to spend time with Trista. There was no talk of sickness, tumors, cancer or any other malady. It was laughing, hugging and the recounting all the funny things that happened when Trista was in the hospital down there.

When it was time for our three visitors to leave, Dr. Rigsby said that it would be difficult for him to get time off, as he had that day, again anytime soon, so he wanted to tell Trista good-bye. We all, including Trista, understood that this wasn't the standard good-bye and the tears welled up in both Trista's and Dr. Rigsby's eyes. They hugged and then the three of them got on the road and headed south.

I can't imagine that this young resident does this type of visit for all of his patients or even a few of them. This special connection could only have been by God's design.

This was the last time that I saw Allison, the nurse who had come to our aid by providing a place for us to stay while Trista took radiation treatments. Allison told me when Trista and I left Nashville that it was likely she and I wouldn't connect again. She was wrong. It's funny how God weaves people in and out of our lives. It can't be by chance but only in reflection of these times does it seem to make any sense at all.

CHAPTER 37

§

BY ALL PHYSICAL INDICATIONS, TRISTA was going to die. It still didn't seem real to me. It seemed like we could still get that healing miracle like the boy had experienced while on the Vanderbilt Hospital elevator. The call we received several days later was one more step toward reality when the Make a Wish Foundation, the organization that provides last wishes for terminally ill children, wanted to know if Trista would like to be a recipient of their program. Very excited, Trista told the organization's representative that for her wish she'd like Michael Jackson or Rick Springfield to come to our house for a visit.

Trista was on an absolute high for days considering the prospect of either of these wishes coming true and was sure every time the phone rang, it would be the Make a Wish people on the other end of the line. Days later the call finally did come and we heard some interesting news. Michael Jackson doesn't visit ill children, they said, and because Rick Springfield is in Australia, he isn't available to visit either. They did, however, provide a third option, which made Trista's eyes get big with excitement as she listened to their proposal.

Because the Mandrel sisters had their own television show, Trista was very familiar with all three famous siblings and their singing talents. Louise Mandrel would be passing through our area in her huge tour bus and offered to visit with Trista on the upcoming Saturday morning. Trista agreed that this was a great plan and handed me the phone to work out the particulars.

We were instructed not to tell anyone that Louise Mandrel was coming to our home, especially not the media. Because this visit was for Trista and our family alone, no one could be in the driveway or our yard, or the bus would not stop. After agreeing to these very reasonable terms, I couldn't wait to tell the rest of the family how we were planning to spend our Saturday.

There was very little sleep going on at our house that Friday night and Trista was ready to get cleaned up to eat very early the next morning. At barely sunrise, I saw a huge bus coming down our little road and it parked in the street because there was no way it would fit in our driveway. Neighbors saw it too and stepped out onto their lawns while still in their pajamas to get a better look. Gratefully, all neighbors were courteous and didn't try to engage Louise Mandrel as this very petite, beautiful brunette exited her huge motor home. Waiting at the door, we invited her inside and introductions were exchanged. After giving Louise a brief summary about Trista's condition, we led her back to the bedroom where Trista was about to pop out of her skin with excitement.

After visiting with our family for well over an hour, Louise discovered that Steph and I sing in church. So she asked if we could sing her a song. We sang several verses of *Though the Mountains May Fall*, with Steph accompanying us on his guitar. We didn't just sing it; we believed those words. "Though the mountains may fall and the hills turn to dust yet the love of the Lord will stand. As a shelter to all who will call on his name, sing the praise and the glory of God." Courteously applauding, Louise smiled and asked if we would like to hear her sing a few songs too. Did she need to ask?

Inviting her guitar player to come inside our home from the bus and with Louise packing her fiddle this time, we knew we were in for a treat. I have no idea what songs she played and sang but I do remember that they made us happy and we were all clapping to the beat. It was fantastic entertainment. Louise is a beautiful person and Trista was having great fun.

Once her concert ended, Louise asked if she could please spend some private time with Trista, just the two of them. So we all left Trista's bedroom in compliance.

There were no sounds coming out of Trista's bedroom for a long time and we couldn't imagine what those two could be discussing. At least half an hour later, Trista's bedroom door opened and Louise stepped into the hall to thank us for letting her come to visit us. With tears in her eyes she headed for the bus and on the way out asked me if I'd like a tour of the inside.

I couldn't believe how big it was inside as Louise took me from room to room. She introduced me to her niece, Barbara Mandrel's daughter, who was traveling with Louise. What a bus! I'd never seen anything so beautiful and efficiently designed to meet all her traveling needs. It was a real house on wheels and I was grateful she let me see the inside.

As I stepped off the last step of the bus stairway, Louise gave me a big hug and then as quietly as it had arrived, the bus drove away. It was as though it all was a dream, or we were a scene in a movie. But it was real and I thought how amazing it was going to be to see The Mandrel Sisters' Show on television next week, knowing that Louise had been here at our house for over three hours.

Walking back into the house and into Trista's room, I couldn't wait to ask Trista what she and Louise talked about when they had been alone with the door closed. Trista said, "Mom, she's really a nice person. She said that she sometimes sings in her church in Nashville. Louise asked me to pray with her and to pray for her. It was wonderful, Mom. I'm so glad she came."

As soon as that bus was out of sight, neighbors rushed to our front porch to get the scoop and we couldn't wait to give it to them. Not much later, a reporter from our local newspaper called to get the scoop too. Trista made the "big-time" news and we all laughed as we kept telling everyone willing to listen the story of Louise Mandrel's visit.

As if this wasn't enough excitement for one week, several days later the phone rang and a man asked to speak to Trista. When I asked who was calling, the voice on the other end responded, "This is Rick Springfield calling from Australia. Could I please speak with Trista?"

After Trista and Rick Springfield had talked for several minutes, she knew we were all anxious to hear what they were saying so Trista held the phone away from her ear so we could hear a little of the conversation too. They conversed about his tour, about Trista's favorite songs he sang and he even asked if she would sing a little of her favorites for him, which she did. They talked for a long time and he made her laugh and swoon at the same time. *What a generous and kind man*, I thought to myself. Trista was so happy and full of life at this moment. She looked so good that if I wasn't able to see her cancer-ravaged body, she would have sounded like any other giddy teenager talking to her singing idol on the phone.

CHAPTER 38

EASTER WAS SOON APPROACHING AND Lent was always a special time for our family. As our Catholic faith encouraged, our family would sometimes give up big things for Lent such as no television for 40 days in order to spend more quality family time together, or we might personally give something up to draw us closer to the Lord and be reminded of the ultimate sacrifice Christ made for us. This particular Lent we decided to not give up anything at all. Trista and her dad volunteered to do a special song together at Easter Mass. Trista would play the flute while her dad would sing and play guitar. This was a celebration of Christ's resurrection and our family was pretty excited and looking forward to celebrating everything, especially being together. Of course, as any woman knows, this calls for a new Easter dress. A light gray and white fabric with a lacy collar and a big sash that tied into a big bow at the back was perfect for Trista. Not too young and not too old, we decided.

Trista and her dad practiced often and Trista seemed to have a burst of wellness throughout these 40 days. Pain was minimal, her disposition was joyful and it was a beautiful time for our family. Because spring was looming and the trees were budding, the landscape even looked hopeful. We all continued to pray that a miracle might really happen.

Holy Week, the week prior to Easter, was always a time we looked forward to observing in our church services. It meant we were just days away from Easter when we would be celebrating with Mass, and of course, lots of Easter candy.

This particular Holy Week, our pastor, Fr. Delma, asked Trista if she would consider representing one of the disciples who would sit in a chair on the altar as Fr. Delma would re-enact Jesus washing the disciples' feet at the Last Supper.

Now Trista wasn't too sure she wanted to do this and she told Fr. Delma she'd think about it. I couldn't imagine what her big dilemma was regarding his request. *Either she wanted to do this, or not do this,* I thought. I had no clue what her concern could be since her only requirements were to have bare feet and sit in the chair.

Shortly after Fr. Delma walked away, Sister Roseanne, a nun who was our Catholic school principal and friend, approached Trista because she knew what our priest had just requested. Sister Roseanne was likely the one assigned to organize the logistics for the foot washing. "Will you do it?" Sister asked. "It all depends," Trista replied. "On what?" Sister asked. "On which disciple I am up there. I will not be Judas no matter what," Trista said. With a big grin on her face, Sister Roseanne assured Trista that she could be John, the disciple Jesus loved. And so, Trista agreed to be a disciple at our church's reenactment of the Last Supper.

The big evening came for the foot washing that was part of our Holy Week service and Trista was ready to assume her role as John. Because Steph had to work that evening, only Trista, Stephan and I attended this Mass but the church was packed with Christ the King parishioners.

Noticing me and my children entering the church, an usher directed us to the front pew where all "disciples" were to be seated in preparation for stepping up to the altar at the proper time. Although I wasn't chosen as a disciple, Stephan and I sat with Trista so I could help direct her onto her "disciple's" seat. She was almost totally blind by this time and none of us were ever far from her in case she needed us.

Finally, the time had come and all the disciples were invited to take their respective seats up at the altar. To ensure that no one would hold up this portion of the service, disciples had removed their shoes and socks in advance. One by one, we watched Fr. Delma washing the feet of the selected parishioners, saying something to each one that was inaudible to the rest of the congregation, then drying the feet and moving onto the next disciple.

It was Trista's turn and as Fr. Delma began washing her feet, Trista began to cry. With big tears streaming down her face, I at first thought she might be getting sick but then realized that wasn't the cause of her emotional downpour. This looked different to me. As our priest spoke softly to her and began to dry her feet, Trista's eyes opened very wide and the tears flowed more rapidly. *What is going on up there?* I wondered. Trista continued to cry throughout her foot washing and throughout the washing of the feet of the two remaining disciples. Finally, it was time to help her down off the sanctuary step and back into her seat at the front pew with me and Stephan.

Because Trista was crying so deeply and could barely catch her breath, it was physically challenging to help her get down the step. A young male parishioner, J.R., saw my dilemma and rushed up to help me. J.R. was visibly moved by Trista's tears, although neither of us knew the cause for them.

Once Trista was again settled in the front row pew I quickly got her a tissue and asked if she was all right, what was wrong and causing her to cry so much. Her reply made the hairs on my arms stand up with a chill as she told me what happened while she was portraying the disciple John.

These were her words as I can best remember them. "I heard Fr. Delma with the person next to me and so I knew I would be next even though I couldn't see what was going on. When Fr. Delma took my feet in his hands to wash them, it wasn't Fr. Delma, it was Jesus. When I realized who it was washing my feet, I didn't know what to say so I just told Him that I loved Him. At this point I was crying too because I believed Trista. I thanked Jesus, praised Him and hugged my dear child who had just been touched by the hands of Jesus. What a gift, a blessing, a holy moment. How could I ever explain this to someone and why should they believe us? *It really doesn't matter if anyone believes us or not*, I thought. God knows.

CHAPTER 39

§

Easter Sunday finally came and our family left early for Mass in great anticipation of a beautiful celebration that included a special song from Trista and her dad. Trista looked lovely in her new Easter dress and young Stephan was quite dapper in his new dress pants and shirt. What a wonderful day!

It was interesting to me that although Trista had lost all of her hair and was almost totally blind, she was completely uninhibited, reaching out to hug or shake the hands of people in church whose voices she knew well.

One man in particular who Trista sought out on Easter Sunday was Garth Gamblin, a man who suffered the disabilities of cerebral palsy. The movement of his arms and legs did not always cooperate and he had extremely distorted speech. Although challenged by his physical impairments, Garth served as editor of a column in our local newspaper that at this time was owned by *The New York Times*.

As our family entered the pew to be seated, Trista could hear Garth talking behind us and turned her body backward to greet him. She boldly asked Garth if she could give him a hug. He responded by struggling to stand and get near her. I remember what a powerful witness this was to me. Trista had gone on her only date with a boy who stuttered severely and now she chose to embrace a man who obviously had spent his lifetime overcoming the trials of his condition. Trista connected with people who struggled, as I'm sure she was struggling to be as normal a teenager as possible with her own physical impairments.

It was almost time for Steph and Trista's special musical number when I noticed Trista's eyes widening as though something was wrong. I had seen this look on her face many times before. After asking her if she was all right, she explained that she needed to go home because she was getting sick, about to have a seizure. She did seize on the way home. Her tears during the ride home weren't due to pain but rather because she felt she had let her dad down. We all assured her this wasn't true.

By the afternoon Trista was feeling better and we continued to celebrate Easter as we had always done with a big meal, great desserts and by chowing down on candy that was overflowing from the kids' Easter baskets.

CHAPTER 40

§

EASTER OF 1984 CAME AND went. As days passed we could see Trista's physical condition begin to further deteriorate. She had lost more weight, slept more, and the pressure in her head caused pain she had not had only weeks before.

Her new attending physician, Dr. Donley, the orthopedic surgeon, told Steph and me that he would help us keep Trista at home so she wouldn't need to go back into the hospital. We were very grateful for that.

It wasn't uncommon that when Dr. Donley was done with his workday at the hospital or office, he would drive by our home and if Trista's bedroom light was on, he'd stop in to see her—sometimes just to sit and talk. His care for her was so loving and kind as he ensured that she experienced as little pain and discomfort as possible. He even taught me how to help Trista when her bowels became impacted. Jim's wife, Judy, a nurse, also supported us with care, prayers and genuine friendship.

At this time our friend Sandy Spera, Trista's former piano teacher who had become a trained hospice volunteer, visited our home more frequently so we would know her support was always available.

Trista seldom left her bed now but on good days she would ask to be wheeled into the living room while lying flat on her wheelchair. It was on one of these occasions in July she came up with another one of her big ideas.

Trista asked if we could have a big prayer meeting in our back-yard. She explained that people could bring picnic lunches and sit on blankets on the grass. Anyone could offer up prayers to God when-ever they wanted to and there could be lots of singing. She wanted our entire Christ the King congregation to be invited.

It was an interesting idea. However, out of concern for Trista's more frequent bouts with pain and weakness, we hesitated. We did agree that we would talk to Fr. Delma about it since he was planning to come to our house for a visit that afternoon.

Trista couldn't wait to share her plan with Fr. Delma. And the plan seemed to grow in detail each time she explained it. After dis-cussion and alignment about our decision as a family, Fr. Delma said he would make the invitation announcement at Mass the week prior to the actual Prayer Meeting date and we would just see if anyone would show up.

It never occurred to me or Steph that so many people would take their Sunday afternoon to sit on the grass in our backyard to attend a prayer meeting. I'm not even certain everyone knew what a prayer meeting was! Unbelievable! The yard was filled with people. Some brought instruments and were prepared to sing. There was enough food to "feed the five thousand" and even our neighbors decided to join the festivities.

Because Trista's bedroom window was open on this beautiful July day, she could hear everything and was absolutely delighted by it all. Steph had taken his sound system and set it up on the patio to ensure that voices could be amplified. The amazing music, sponta-neous prayers, children laughing, kept a smile on Trista's face as she laid in her bed listening with eyes closed.

After several hours of this backyard praise celebration, one of our friends knocked on Trista's bedroom door and Trista invited him to come in. He told Trista that everyone outside was asking where she was and that they wanted her to join them outside, even for just a few minutes.

Trista's response to his request wasn't anything I expected. She told the man how happy she was that everyone came. Then she said: "Please tell everyone that I won't be coming outside at all. Right now everyone is praising God and if I go outside, their attention will be on me. Thank them for coming and tell them I love them." Our friend then went outside to share what Trista had said. In response to her message for them, there was more praising God and more spontaneous prayers.

What a day this was for us all to see Trista's vision of a prayer meeting realized. As her condition continued to worsen, she told the story of this day to many people and recounted many times what took place in our backyard.

CHAPTER 41

§

MORE DAYS PASSED, AND WITH each day came an interesting series of events. The first was a visit from a former salon client who had recently become a Christian. In her eagerness to live this new life in Christ she said she was compelled/driven, to visit our family and hoped we would allow it. Not knowing this woman's agenda for her visit, I decided she was likely harmless and probably just wanted to pray for Trista. However, I decided it would be prudent of me to have a conversation with her before allowing her to spend time with my daughter, whom she had never met. This cautionary inclination of mine had to be a "God thing," because I listened in horror as she detailed her Christian duty to help our family.

The woman stepped through our doorway with a gift of a bottle of wine and a friendly hug. Not remembering this woman to be a hugger, it was uncomfortable for me to hug her. It felt like I was hugging an actor in a role taken from a well-rehearsed script.

After being seated in our living room, the woman explained that she was certain she knew the cause of Trista's illness and what could be done for her to receive healing. Fully engaged by her enthusiasm at this point, I listened intently as she shared her perspective of her new spiritual insight. Looking me straight in the eyes she said, "Trista is sick because of sin. It could be your sin, her sin or the sin of a family member. You need to ask God the nature of this sin, by whom, and confess it and then ask for Trista's healing."

Totally caught off guard by her words and glancing at her gift of the bottle of wine, I calmly responded. "Thank you for your good intentions by coming here, but you need to leave our home now." Standing up and walking toward our front door myself so that she understood I was serious, she quickly followed my example and stood, then headed for the front door. Undeterred and in perfect peace about what she had shared, the woman again hugged me, to which I again cringed inside. She then promptly left.

Stung by her words and reeling to consider if there was a fraction of truth in them, I just stood beside the door in almost a trance. Trista's voice broke this trance as she called to me from her room.

We have a saying in our family, "Tell the truth no matter who it hurts." In her straight forwardness and totally transparent way, Trista did just that. "Mom, who was that crazy woman you were talking to? And why did you let her in our house? I'm so glad you told her to leave. Never let her back in here!" she said. I was in complete agreement with Trista's assessment of this situation. I probably should have prayed for that woman and I still have not.

On another occasion, Fr. Delma called to ask us if a family he had just met could come to visit Trista. You can imagine that after this last incident I had become reluctant to allow people I didn't know well to gain entrance into our home. This seemed like a strange request to me. Not understanding why this family that he had just met would want to come visit us, I had to ask more questions before saying yes. I also needed to confer with Trista to be sure she was signed up for such a visit.

Fr. Delma shared the story with us. This family, that included a mom, dad and two disabled children, just showed up on his rectory doorstep. Because the dad was out of work, they were destitute. They had been traveling from town to town looking for employment opportunities to support the family. When this family had stopped in town at a place prior to coming to the rectory, someone had shared the story about Trista's illness with them. In reflection this also may have been about the time that Garth Gamlin, the newspaper columnist I spoke about earlier, wrote an article that appeared in the local paper telling about how a multitude of people had come to the aid of our family. No matter how the dad learned about Trista, he asked Fr. Delma if he would contact us to see if their family could meet her.

Knowing that Fr. Delma would never intentionally put our family in harm's way and trusting in his spiritual discernment about people, I asked him what he thought we should do. It was a quick and definite response from him, "Let them come, Shirley. I don't think you'll be sorry." After Trista agreed to the visit, I called Fr. Delma to ask the family if they would like to come on over to our house.

Not having any idea what to expect, I watched our driveway through the living-room window and cautiously observed a very badly beat-up old car pull in. Out from this broken-down vehicle poured the dad and mom who then assisted their children to our front door. One child, about seven years old, was obviously mentally handicapped while the other child, much younger, was physically impaired. Although very shabbily dressed in ill-fitting clothes, I noticed that all four were clean and smiling as they walked through our front door. "We came to see Trista, please," the dad said. It was at this moment that I just knew it was all right to have these people come in.

Although Trista couldn't see them, they introduced themselves and told her how difficult their lives had been. They weren't complaining, just stating the facts. We all listened intently as the father shared how badly he needed to get a job to care for his family. They were a beautiful family who seemed very loving to each other. Because the disabled children were so well-behaved, it seemed somewhat abnormal. They were smiling and just checking out Trista's room as any typical children would do under the circumstances.

After the father was done sharing his story, Trista, one to always cut to the chase, said, "So did you come to pray over me for healing?" To which the father responded, "No, I've come to ask you to pray over us." Tears welled up in Trista's eyes, a major grin crossed her face, and she shared, "This is a special day. You have asked for prayer from me instead of coming to pray over me! Let's pray." As the family bowed their heads, Trista prayed so softly that I'm not sure what she said. I do remember tears in the father's eyes as he seemed to digest each of her words like food nourishing his body and giving him strength. At the end of this prayer, everyone said a big, *"AMEN."*

After thanking Trista for her prayers, the family left our home and we never saw them again. I guess they were truly just passing through as the father had said. Having this family in our home was a huge gift, a true blessing for us all, especially for Trista.

We couldn't wait to call Fr. Delma and thank him for sending this family to us. Trista never told us what she said when she prayed over them. I don't believe she ever mentioned this family again. But on this day, God most certainly used an indigent family to nourish Trista's soul and ours.

CHAPTER 42

§

NOT LONG AFTER THE VISIT by the indigent family came a couple from our church who were also quite poor, but not homeless. Steph and I met this man and his wife through Fr. Delma who connected the four of us to praise and pray together weekly. Reminding me of Johnny Cash, this man played a few guitar chords and sang several songs of praise which I grew to cherish as preparation for prayer. One song had as the lyrics, "Let's forget about ourselves, magnify the Lord and praise His name." As our new friend sang these words, we knew they were sung honestly and sincerely.

One day, this couple invited us to their home for dinner. Wondering how they could afford a meal for us as well as themselves, I eagerly asked what we could bring. "Pop," the wife said.

Journeying down a long dirt road following the directions they'd given us to their home, we came upon a small old trailer sitting in the middle of nowhere with no other homes or trailers anywhere around it. I was glad the weather was decent and the sun wouldn't set for hours so we would be able to find our way back out of there. We were greeted by two big welcoming smiles and hearty handshakes.

I wondered if this couple had invited others to dinner before or if they just felt comfortable with us because of our weekly praise and prayer sessions together. I also began to consider that God had given them what some called, "the gift of hospitality." I knew this gift had nothing to do with financial status. I knew that they were special people who loved God and I loved them for it. I was very glad we came.

They invited us to step into their home using a gesture directing us through the front door. It was instantly easy to see that this family was having some tough economic times. There was a big hole in the front door and a portion of the front door screen had been ripped off. They then suggested that we go back outside where we would enjoy our dinner together.

We could see that the man had done some serious physical work, by the size of the logs, to build this giant bonfire that we hadn't noticed when we first arrived. Handing each of us a stick that was pre-whittled to a point at one end, we were directed to impale our own hotdogs for cooking over this huge fire. What fun, I thought! Along with the hotdog we had our glass of pop. I thanked God for this beautiful couple who so graciously invited us to their home.

Later this same couple came to our home to visit Trista. The wife was always joyful and smiling. As a hairdresser I couldn't help but notice her jet black hair that was similar to the hair coloring Elvis Presley must have used. I truly loved this couple and was glad they came.

The wife approached Trista who was in her bed to ask how she was doing. Trista replied her standard, "I'm fine."

After a typical conversational exchange about our families among us all, the wife asked if she could pray over Trista and Trista gave her consent.

Both husband and wife knelt on the floor on either side of Trista's bed and with eyes closed and hands reaching up to heaven. They quickly began praising God and thanking Him for all kinds of things like His love, grace and power within us. Suddenly their prayers went to a different dialect that neither Trista nor I had ever before heard. Suspecting they were praying in tongues, we listened but had no earthly idea what they were saying.

The very second their prayers ended, Trista said to them, "What was that? What were you both saying?" Completely filled with joy, the wife couldn't wait to tell us about how she and her husband were praying in their prayer language. She explained that the prayer language is a gift from God that anyone who loves Jesus can ask for and receive. She added that when they don't know how to pray, the Holy Spirit takes over what they are saying so that they are praying the perfect prayer in God's will every single time.

Intrigued by this explanation, Trista smiled implying she liked what the woman had just said. So the woman asked if Trista would also like to receive this gift. "Yes!" Trista responded excitedly. At this point the couple laid their hands on Trista and began to pray over her. It all happened so fast that I was personally caught a bit off guard. I stood there at the foot of her bed observing what was happening. Not particularly knowledgeable about speaking in tongues, as it is sometimes called, I could not imagine these prayers to God as anything harmful, so I said nothing. Knowing Trista to be completely truthful and precocious, I knew she would never pretend or want to pretend receiving this gift if she really hadn't.

Out they gushed from our daughter's mouth as rapidly and with as much force as an eruption from Old Faithful—words indistinguishable to my ears. The couple, totally filled with gratitude to God, just looked up and laughed. They thanked Him repeatedly.

When Trista finished praying this way, her only response was, "Cool!" Without missing a beat, Trista then asked the couple to pray over me, too. They did, but nothing happened. Seemingly unconcerned, the wife shared that my prayer language would come in God's time and her comment took the pressure off me. I knew I had nothing to do with receiving this gift on my own and was grateful for her confirmation of that.

This couple, who we not only enjoyed and now admired for their faith and courage, left our home. Trista never saw them again, but she didn't really need to. Her gift was given and received through them. They had shared a powerful new prayer venue and we were all, especially Trista, grateful that God sent them into our lives for this very moment.

§

CHAPTER 43

As the days progressed, Trista began to speak more often about going to heaven, especially when she began having challenges eating. Because she had no appetite and her stomach often hurt, I believe that she merely attempted to eat to please us.

It wasn't uncommon for me to lay in bed with Trista and talk to her by whispering into her ear. She seemed to like that even though it continued to be painful for her to be touched or hugged. She now had only one hand that she could control.

One day seemed particularly difficult for me to keep a cheery disposition and Trista must have sensed it although I tried to hide it. She asked me how I was doing and I told her, "Just fine." I knew that she didn't believe me when she said, "You know what you need, Mom? You need a big hug from me. Come on over here by my good arm so I can give you a big hug." The dam of my resolve could no longer hold the stored-up tears as I lay encircled by her one remaining working arm. I couldn't stop crying. It was on this day that Trista decided it was time to get her affairs in order so she would be ready to see Jesus. *What possible affairs in order?* I thought. She asked me to take notes about which things she needed my help to complete.

Trista's first order of business was to ask Fr. Delma to come over to the house for her to make her confession. She was adamant about not having any sin that she could remember be on her soul. What could she have done that I didn't know about? She had truly been an obedient child who lived to please her parents. I talked with Fr. Delma who said he'd be over the following day.

Because this was a true confession—the Sacrament of Reconciliation—Trista and Fr. Delma needed complete privacy. The door to her bedroom was closed out of respect for this gift.

It seemed like such a long time had passed but finally the door opened and we were invited back into her room. Just before Fr. Delma turned to leave, he said to Trista, "When you get to heaven will you pray for me, Trista?" Trista laughed out loud and said, "What makes you think that I'll get to heaven before you do? Only God knows that. You could be killed in a car wreck going back up the hill to the rectory." We all cracked up in laughter at this, including Fr. Delma, because what Trista had said was certainly true.

Shortly after Fr. Delma left, Trista asked me to get her bank out of her closet. It was bright red and in the shape of a mailbox. It even had a flag to pull up or down. I retrieved it and she asked me to remove the $100 bill from it that I didn't even know she had. Explaining that someone who had visited her a while back had given it to her and she had placed it in her bank until she could decide what to do with it. After I put the bill into her hand, Trista handed it back to me and asked me to please accept it from her so that her soul would be clean. I didn't understand why. Trista explained that before she had gotten sick, I had asked her to greet customers at the reception desk at our salon on a Saturday. Trista had stolen $20 from the till that I never knew about. She said that scripture required her to pay back five times what she had stolen and that would be $100. She was so serious about this debt being paid that I had to accept the money. Check. The first of her tasks were completed.

The next few tasks on her list had to do with having one-on-one conversations with specific members of our family. First on the list was her Uncle Greg, who lived two houses away from ours. Summoned and now seated by her bed and holding her hand, Greg could never have envisioned what Trista was about to say to him.

I must share a little review of our family background here for context. Greg is my husband's brother. Greg's wife, Pam, is my sister. That makes all of our children double cousins. Because our two families were so entwined, we were really close and hung out together. Greg and Pam had just had their third child, Elliot, so Trista's Aunt Pam was caring for a newborn while we were caring for Trista.

Trista, true to the family motto, "Tell the truth no matter who it hurts," lovingly said to her Uncle Greg, "Uncle Greg, do you love my Aunt Pam?" To which Greg, with a puzzled look on his face replied, "Yes." "Then you need to be nicer to her," Trista replied. Unbelievably uncomfortable and likely believing Trista was affected by drugs to a state of dementia, Greg gave Trista a patronizing smile, then said nothing more as he continued to hold her hand. Trista knew her Uncle Greg loved her and he graciously accepted what she said out of his love for her. Check. Task number two completed.

Because Trista enjoyed a very close relationship with both her dad and brother, Stephan, she gave me special instructions for each of them. Knowing her brother's independent nature, she asked me to keep a very close eye on Stephan and protect him. When about to speak to me concerning her dad, she put her head down and shared that he would have a very difficult time after she was gone and I needed to take special care of him. I didn't really know what she meant by this at the time but I agreed to do as she had asked.

With Trista's two major tasks completed she said it was time for her to plan her funeral. Playing along because it seemed to please her, I began to take notes as she shared the following. "I need a Baptist song for Puppa and Grandma." They were my parents. "I think *When the Roll is Called up Yonder*, will be perfect," she said. "Next, I want a special song for the Blessed Mother so I can thank her. *Gentle Woman* would be nice." I asked, " Is there a special song for you?" She thought for a moment and said that her song would be *Son of David Have Mercy on Me*. "After these songs," she added, "you can put in any other songs you want".

The women who worked in our beauty salon, which included Trista's godmother Tara, asked if they could provide the dress for Trista to wear when she would see Jesus. As hesitant as I was to even ask Trista about this request, she was delighted about this idea and asked if she could pick the dress out. I wasn't sure how well this would work out since Trista was blind. I shared her request with Tara.

Several days passed before Tara and Marge arrived at the house to show Trista several dresses from which she could pick her favorite. Each of the women got down on their knees as they told Trista about each dress's color, style and description. They then let her feel the fabric. Listening intently, it was as though Trista was trying to visualize what each dress looked like. Several dresses had been described and held in Trista's hands to further examine when Tara and Marge described another dress that seemed to really catch Trista's attention. While feeling the fabric she asked, "Is there a design on this one? What is the design?" Holding the fabric closer so she could see the design more clearly, Tara said, "I think those are tiny butterflies. Yes, they're tiny little butterflies. Butterflies are a sign of the Risen Lord!" Delighted, Trista said definitively, "That's my dress I'll wear to see Jesus!" I remember that some of those dresses that had been brought over were expensive. However, the one Trista chose had been marked down numerous times and now cost $12.99. Check. This task completed!

CHAPTER 44

§

WITH ALL OF THE TASKS on Trista's list completed, she was at peace. She spoke and ate a little less each day. Her wilting body was tinier and frail, and yet, she made great use of the one good arm as she wrapped it around numerous people to give them big hugs.

After bathing Trista one morning, she asked me if I would pray for her to go be with Jesus. Explaining that she was tired and ready to go, Trista asked if we could pray together this way and I responded, "No." As her mom, I could not ask God to take her. I just couldn't.

Several days passed and with Trista unable to eat at all, I asked Dr. Donley if we should get her a feeding tube to which Trista said, "No way, Mom. Please don't."

How could I starve my child? How could I continue to watch her body whither and not try to nourish her in some way? This seemed so wrong to me but Trista was adamant that to keep her here when she was ready to go was wrong, too. She finally said to me, "Mom, if you really love me, you'll let me go." I remembered that these were the exact words she used when she wanted to attend the Louisville School for the Blind. What she said was true and on that day we prayed together for her to be able to go see Jesus as tears streamed down both of our faces.

We all knew as a family that God would take her soon. Dr. Donley told us that Trista would likely go into a coma for a while before passing on. Knowing this, I wouldn't leave her except to go to the bathroom. Sleeping on the floor of her bedroom, I spent each night just listening to her breathe. Because I have big ears, my hearing had always been keen and I thanked God for that gift.

Each of us, wanting to have special conversations with her, took turns talking with her. But one conversation she had with her dad is one I'll always remember."Trista," he said, "When you get to heaven will you give me a sign that you're okay?" "I'm not sure how that all works, but if I can, I will," she assured him. How important it is for dads to know that their little girls are all right. This conversation with Trista made me realize that this never stops, not even in death.

CHAPTER 45

§

ONE DAY, TRISTA WAS BECOMING increasingly uncomfortable in her bed. No position was working for her and we were challenged to know how to help her. Bedsores were beginning to appear even though we moved her body often. Never complaining, she let us treat the sores. I think more for us than for her. Nevertheless, she was in extreme discomfort.

A knock suddenly came at the door and I went to answer it when I saw before me a beautiful African American woman—probably in her thirties—standing on the porch. "Yes?" I said. With a big beautiful smile on her face, she introduced herself and asked if she could come inside to sing Trista a song. *A strange request*, I thought. Not knowing this woman but also reflecting on the fact that some unusual blessings had come to us from visitors we didn't know, I unlocked the screen door and held up one finger to signal to the woman that I'd be right back.

Once in Trista's room, I explained the situation and asked Trista what she thought we should do. She said, "Mom, let her in." And so with only me, my mom and Trista at home, we invited this total stranger into Trista's bedroom. The song she sang so beautifully was *His Eye Is On the Sparrow*. I remember how this woman's very presence made me feel. It was as though an angel came into our home. Her voice was more lovely than any voice I had ever heard. She celebrated with her words how God cares for every detail of our lives.

It was as though we had been praying day in and day out and God sent this messenger to assure us that He heard all of our petitions.

Not wanting the song to be over because we were entranced by her and her words, I was a little sad when she was done. She thanked us and quickly left. I watched as she walked down our Winding Creek Trail until she was out of sight.

For several days I asked neighbors who would pop in if they knew this woman or who she might be. We got the same answer each time we asked, "We've never heard her name and I'm sure that no African American women live in our neighborhood."

I didn't need an explanation and neither did Trista or my mom. To us, that woman was an angel. For His eye is on the sparrow and I know He watches me. That is all we needed to know.

CHAPTER 46

§

THE FOLLOWING DAY BEGAN WITH me waking up from my bed on the floor to hear Trista yelling. Thinking she might be in pain, I popped up quickly to investigate. No, it wasn't anything to do with pain. She was just angry, angry with God! Trista explained that she was ready to go be with Jesus. We had prayed for it, and she wanted to know why He wasn't answering her prayers. Trista was upset because she woke up to another day still in her bed! "Get Fr. Delma right away," she ordered. And I did.

I don't know what our priest said to calm her down, but it worked and our home was once again peaceful, yet watchful. We truly wanted Trista to feel at peace going to Jesus and yet we were fearful for that to actually happen.

I decided it was time for me to get as physically close to Trista as possible, to lie beside her in her bed and gently put my arm around her so she would feel me near her. Whether this was more for me or for her, I don't know. But to have her slip away from us while I was out of the room to grab a bite or go to the bathroom was frightening to me and totally unacceptable.

I could feel her tiny body slightly lifting my arm ever so gently up and down with every short breath. It was quiet, restful, and we were content to be in this moment that went on throughout that day and into the night.

I remember sharing my fear of not being with Trista when she died with Fr. Delma. In his usual calm, peaceful manner he let me know that Trista didn't need me or anyone else to go to heaven, only Jesus. And He would provide everything, be everything. Although our pastor's words rang true to me, I realized it was me who desperately needed to be with Trista when she left this earth. I was there when God gave her to us in birth and I, as her mom, wanted to be there when He took her back. It wasn't nearly long enough—almost 14 years. It went too fast. For some unknown reason I began to reflect on all the bad things I had ever said or done. I envisioned Trista getting to heaven and being capable of seeing and knowing how many times I failed to be kind or do what was right. Fear struck me. Trista would know all my faults and might not be proud of me as her mother.

What a selfish thought—all about me. I committed my mind to keep these kinds of thoughts away and focus on my dying child—her needs, her life and the fact that she was slipping away right in front of me.

Night came and sometime into the night Trista became very restless, seemingly no longer weak but rather filled with strength to maneuver her weak body all over her bed. Due to her continued uneasiness, I went back to my bed on the floor at the foot of her bed. It was dark and quiet. At first I thought I was dreaming as sounds of moaning touched my ears. I heard whispers at first, then louder sounds at almost normal volume like a one-on-one conversation. I got up to see what was going on. I realized that Trista was indeed engaged in a conversation, but her words were not recognizable to me because they were similar to what I had heard her say when speaking her new prayer language. Over and over she spoke the sounds and phrasing, even at times sounding like she was arguing with someone. Lying back down and now listening from my bed on the floor, this conversation went on throughout the balance of the night. Unable to sleep, not permitting myself to doze off at all, her talking went on and on then suddenly stopped. Fearful I had missed her passing, I climbed back into her bed and again placed my arm around her body where I could feel her breath move my arm up and down. Although her breathing was very shallow, she breathed. I thanked God for her breath as I cried as silently as possible. This time Trista gave no response to my tears.

She lay quietly, peacefully, as though there was no more need for any talking. *It could have been that she was listening, waiting*, I thought. I know she could still hear me because I whispered into her ear and she squeezed my arm with her good hand. I thanked God that she could hear me as I remembered the doctors saying Trista would likely go into a coma for an undetermined length of time before she would die. This was no coma, just silence.

As sunlight announced the morning by creeping through her bedroom curtain, nothing had changed except her breathing seemed more difficult. She was struggling to catch each breath. It seemed longer between each breath and sometimes she would slightly gasp to catch the breath she had missed. Her dad, noticing Trista's struggle, suggested that we call Dr. Donley so he could get some oxygen ordered for her. As though Trista was startled by an alarm clock, her eyes widened and she loudly responded, "Hun uh," signaling a loud "no" in the only way she was able to now communicate.

Trista was ready to go. To put her through dragging out this process would have been wrong. Both Steph and I clearly knew Trista's wishes and I told her that there would be no oxygen ordered. At this point her body was again relaxed even though she continued to struggle to breathe.

Lying next to her, her body was so warm and soft. I knew that if God wanted Trista to get well, even at this stage of her illness, He could do it. But He didn't. He was, however, giving her great peace and I knew that she knew exactly what was happening. Every few minutes or so I softly whispered into her ear that I loved her. After each time that I said this, she would squeeze my arm that was wrapped around her.

Never having experienced how it is to be with someone at the point of their death, I had no idea what to expect. Should someone offer some kind of lesson about this so that those attending such an important event could be prepared to best support the loved one who is leaving? What if I do something wrong or miss an important moment? There is no way to do it over. What does she really need from me, her mother? What does she need from any of us attending so near her?

The wisdom of Fr. Delma came to my mind once again, "Trista doesn't need your help to get to heaven." I also reflected on Trista's visit from the Blessed Mother standing in the fifth- floor window while she was at Vanderbilt Hospital. The Mother of Jesus, our Lord, told Trista she would never leave her and not to be afraid. Clearly, Trista was not afraid. As Trista had told us when it was revealed that she might not live, she always knew from the time she was diagnosed by Dr. Brewer that she wouldn't survive this cancer. Her concern was for us, the ones she would leave behind.

It had been 18 months since that diagnosis and all the time between that day and now seemed as though it had been preparation for this very moment. It was for this moment that God worked out in us what we would need. Jesus was born for the purpose of His suffering, death and resurrection. We are all born, in His image, to glorify God and then die to live in all eternity with Him.

Eternity? I can't get my arms around eternity, but I do have my arm around my dear child who will be leaving us soon.

§

CHAPTER 47

WATCHING TRISTA'S ILLNESS PROGRESS, DAY after day, was incredibly difficult for her younger brother Stephan. We had tried to ensure Stephan kept as normal a routine and schedule as possible. What does "normal routine" under these circumstances mean for a 12-year-old boy who is going through the stages of trying to make sense of his raging hormones that are causing his body to suddenly grow taller, his voice to get lower?

Thinking that we needed to protect our young son from the visible evidence of the wasting away of his sister's body, we encouraged Stephan to go on a scouting trip to Canada with his troop. Since one of Stephan's good friends, Chris, who lived down the street, was also going, Stephan agreed. My rationale was that Stephan could be doing physical activities outdoors with boys his age. Because Stephan was high strung, filled with energy, this would give him an escape from the trauma we were all living as we watched Trista slowly die, day after day.

Never believing that Trista would leave us this soon, Stephan was canoeing in the wilderness where Canadian mosquitoes were fighting each other for access to any available exposed skin on his body. A part of me believed that the prediction about Trista's coma might still happen.

It came and went as softly as a butterfly gently landing on the petal of a flower in the summer sun, her last breath. If my arm hadn't been around her body and my lips not near her ear, I might have missed it. "She stopped breathing," I said aloud. I checked the rise and fall of my arm because I might have been wrong. It was confirmed. As though we had rehearsed and mastered our roles as characters in a play, both Steph and I looked up at exactly the same time and said, "Thank you," to thank God for her life and now her entrance into heaven.

Death, Trista's death, did not frighten me or cause me to pull my body away from hers. My arm stayed snuggly wrapped around her and my lips on her ear. I did not want to let her go and so I continued to hold my dear child, knowing full well that she was no longer there.

I don't know how long I stayed in that position, holding her while she lay in her bed but I do remember her doctor coming into the room. Someone must have called him. Dr. Donley was there to officially pronounce her time of death. *I will hold her as long as I can*, I thought. My mom came into the room to tell me it was time to let Trista go. Reluctantly I lifted myself away from her. Dr. Donley needed to do something to her body. I didn't want to watch so I left the room. It was all right that I leave because my daughter was gone and only her body lay there now.

Stepping into the living room I saw Tara, Trista's godmother, who said nothing and just hugged me. Then, suddenly, the most excruciating headache came like an intruder with a vengeance. It was so painful that I didn't think I could bear it. After Tara communicated my problem to Dr. Donley, he instructed her to give me one teaspoon of Trista's morphine and, then to pour the remainder of the bottle into the commode and flush. She did as instructed and almost immediately, my pain was gone. Never having taken morphine, I had no frame of reference as to what it would do to me or how it would make me feel. All it did was knock the headache out and I realized how someone who was in constant pain could become addicted to such a drug. Thankful for the relief, we all moved on to the protocol of taking Trista's sheet-covered body, now laying on the gurney, out of the house and into the ambulance. I assumed her body would be taken to the funeral home, but wasn't sure.

I can't say for sure what happened shortly after her body was taken. I do remember asking for my son, Stephan. His dad and I were reserved and somewhat withdrawn at this time but totally in tune with each other's thinking. We needed our son home with us immediately! It would require emergency communication to get him back from Canada and I asked someone to do whatever it takes to get him with us as quickly as possible.

With that request in motion, it was time to call Steph's parents, Grandpa and Grandma France, to let them know Trista was gone. In hindsight, I believe the effects of the morphine enabled me to peacefully manage my response to them inquiring if they really needed to come down to Kentucky for the funeral. "My sweetheart's legs give her terrible pain when she rides too long in the car," my father-in-law explained. My calm reply was, "Do whatever you need to do. We just wanted you to know that she's gone."

I knew that my mom had already contacted my dad, Trista's Puppa. Because my dad and Trista were so close and even though he couldn't bear watching her decline, I knew he'd be making the nine-hour drive from Akron to be with us all. I think that he must have held his tears for every minute of those nine hours because once he stepped into the door of our home, he released a flood of grieving tears.

A rush of food came to our home that day. *How did they prepare it so quickly?* I thought. Who is going to eat all of this food? *This grieving family isn't hungry. Maybe the food is for all the people who come to provide comfort*, I thought. That is how it was served up and ultimately consumed.

CHAPTER 48

§

As I MENTIONED EARLIER, THE very idea of Trista's body being in a funeral home was upsetting to me. The plan was that her body would be brought to our church several hours before the funeral so that people could come to pray in lieu of any sort of traditional visitation or viewing of her body. Since Trista was adamant about the prayer meeting in our backyard being totally focused on God rather than her, we were certain she would have agreed with this arrangement.

Time sped forward to the day of Trista's funeral and I was thankful that our son was again safely home with us. Several hours before we were planning to leave for the church, Sister Ann, a nun from our parish, stopped at our home to spend a few minutes with me. Because Sister Ann had tutored our son Stephan in math while Trista was sick, she was quite familiar with the journey our family was taking. In her kindness, she asked me if I was able to celebrate Trista's new life in Christ rather than mourn my loss. I listened as she asked if I could wear a bright- colored dress to Trista's funeral. I explained that my head knew what she was saying was correct but my heart was so heavy that I needed to be authentic in the black I had laid out on my bed to wear.

I knew that the spiritual maturity of Sister Ann far exceeded my own. I was thankful for the impact she made on the lives of my family. She broadened our perspectives of how we thought about God when she was in our home. She also facilitated what she called

"Awareness Classes" for our salon staff each Monday morning for a while. I'm not certain that I fully grasped or was able to apply the content of what she offered us in those classes at the time, but the context of why we were learning it made perfect sense to me. Her goal was always to draw us nearer to God.

Sister Ann continued to speak to me about celebrating Trista's new life, no matter what I chose to wear. This beautiful nun definitely believed that Trista trusted God fearlessly and her mortal death was a new beginning, never an end. Her words were lovely but I struggled to digest them fully. I just hugged her and thanked her for her thoughtfulness and boldness to share these truths with me at this time. I knew she loved us.

Surprisingly, once Sister Ann left, another visitor arrived on our front porch. It looked like someone familiar but I couldn't remember how I knew her. A beautiful and quite energetic woman—probably in her early thirties--gave me a big smile. She asked if she could come into the house to speak to me for a minute. Assuming that just about everyone in our small town likely knew what was going on with our family, I let her in. It is still amazing to me how freely people, sometimes complete strangers, came and went in our home ever since Trista got sick. Our typical "on guard to potential harm" muscle totally dismantled, we just kept letting these people not only into our home but into our lives. Certain that God sent each one, we sort of gave up worrying about potential dangerous repercussions typically associated with strangers.

So in she came, so full of life and grinning from ear to ear. After she introduced herself as a member of the local Presbyterian Church, the church where I had given the Walk to Emmaus retreat talk, she excitedly handed me a check, for an amount I no longer remember. "What's this?" I asked. "Our Walk to Emmaus Community understood that your family's finances have been depleted because of Trista's illness. We all prayed about it and know that God wants us to buy Trista's tombstone. After checking into it, this is the money collected that we believe should cover the cost. Please don't turn us down, Shirley. We have absolutely no way to give this money back and all the people that donated believe that their money will be used for this purpose."

Standing there, looking at this check in total disbelief, I shared with this woman that I didn't know what to say to her or these people who gave their money. How could these people have possibly known that several days earlier my dad asked if we had made any arrangement for Trista's tombstone to be placed on her grave at the Akron cemetery plot he had given us. Not knowing where the money would come from, I answered my dad with a simple "no" and figured we could put the tombstone up later. The $4000 we received from Trista's life insurance went toward the funeral home bill. There wasn't any money left.

Still unsure what to say to this woman, I said nothing at all. With tears streaming down my face I simply hugged her. Responding to me with another one of her big grins, she hugged me back firmly then immediately headed outside toward her car.

It was quiet in the house now as we were getting dressed to go to Trista's funeral at Christ the King Church just up the hill. No one spoke and that seemed to be a comfortable environment. What was left to say? God even made sure that Trista's tombstone would be provided for through some people we did know and some we did not. *Only God could do such a thing* I thought, then off we went.

CHAPTER 49

§

IT WAS SURREAL SITTING IN the front pew with Trista's casket to my immediate left. It was 30 minutes before Mass was scheduled to begin and I didn't care who was in attendance. I didn't check to see who was or wasn't there. It didn't matter to me. But I did hear a stir of people suddenly start talking so I glanced back toward the front door of the church to see what was happening. Coming down the aisle was my tiny and very unsteady-looking Uncle Bill, Dad's brother, along with my Aunt Rossie and Uncle Harold, another one of dad's brothers and his wife. They had all come from Bloomington, Indiana.

The five siblings in my family had always been closer to my dad's brothers and sisters than my mom's. This was probably because they lived closer to us—a doable driving distance. Steph and I, wanting our children to know these very special aunts and uncles, also took our children to Indiana to see them. However, we were more attached and completely partial to Uncle Carl, Uncle Bill, Uncle Harold and Aunt Rossie. We would take our kids to stay at Uncle Harold and Aunt Rossie's home. Like my parents, all these loving Stewart relatives had tremendous appreciation for the simple and most ordinary gifts in life such as beautiful gardens and robust, ridiculously funny conversations. What a loving and rich heritage we enjoyed with these loving Hoosiers.

Uncle Bill was a school bus driver and a simple farmer who would ask my dad for two one-dollar bills. Uncle Bill would then give my sister and me each one of these dollars if we would agree to kiss him on the cheek. This would make everyone laugh.

Aunt Rossie and Uncle Harold always grew the most beautiful flowers and relished opportunities to teach us about each flower in their yard. Not surprisingly, Uncle Harold's field was education. Helping others learn just ran through those Stewart boys' veins.

I loved these relatives but had no expectation that they would come so far to be with us this day. Rising from the front pew, I flew to hug and greet them while crying and realizing what a physical sacrifice it had been for them to be here.

Trista's casket was closed but something in me wanted these dear relatives, as well as young Stephan, to see her one last time to say good-bye. I asked that the casket be opened briefly, then closed for the last time. Maybe *I* needed one more glance. It seemed right.

All were seated and Fr. Delma was standing at the altar along with two male musicians with whom my husband often sang at Mass. These musicians were leading the singing for the song Trista had chosen for my parents, *When the Roll is Called Up Yonder*, although it clearly was not part of their repertoire. It was perfect nonetheless and then it was time for the homily or sermon.

I did not have a clue what Fr. Delma was going to say. I was thankful that this sermon would not be a general one. He had known Trista well. He not only knew her but was also her friend, her confidante and confessor. She loved Fr. Delma and he knew it. I knew that his message would be real, authentic and personal.

Fr. Delma spoke about how it was before Trista was born and still in my womb. He said that she loved it in there before her birth where she was always cared for and loved. She really did not want to leave that place inside of me. Nevertheless, he said, once she was born, if you had asked her if she'd like to go back into my womb, she would have said, "No." Fr. Delma went on to say that Trista loved life, our family, school, music, her friends, but now that she's with Jesus, she'd again tell us that she wouldn't want to come back. Somehow, this was comforting to me as her mom. As I reflected on this message, I knew it was true. Trista had asked us to pray with her, that God would take her to Himself very soon. She definitely would not want to come back. With Jesus she was healed, cared for and loved in a way we can't even comprehend. I know this. Yet, my heart ached so badly for her that it caused me constant physical pain and I wasn't sure I could bear it.

It was time for the recessional hymn and because the musicians needed one more song they selected one called, *Here I Am, Lord*. I had never before heard it. Some of the words included, "Here I am, Lord. Is it I, Lord? I have heard you calling in the night. I will go Lord, if you lead me. I will hold your people in my heart." What a perfect song choice. How grateful I was for those words.

CHAPTER 50

§

THE FUNERAL ENDED AND OUR family headed north to Akron, Ohio. We traveled in our cars for the nine hours to where Trista would be buried. I wasn't made aware of how Trista's casket would get there until Fr. Delma told me that a parishioner from our church who owned a private plane would be flying her body, him and Sandy, our hospice volunteer. We would all meet at the gravesite at the scheduled time. The parishioner who owned the plane asked to remain anonymous. We were never told his identity and were unable to thank him.

We caravanned down the highway—three cars which included our family, my sister's family and my parents. The drive was uneventful and quiet for over an hour. Suddenly we began noticing butterflies, first just flying near the car, then in front of the car, then smacking into the windshield. We had never seen anything like this. *Going 65 miles an hour, how could this happen?* It was so unlikely an event that the three of us in our car started laughing about it because by this time Steph needed to turn on his windshield wipers to remove the butterflies that were obstructing his view to drive.

We could see up ahead that there was a Long John Silver's restaurant near Elizabethtown and we decided that this would be a good place to get a beverage and take a bio break. Still bewildered by the butterfly situation, Steph turned off at the exit and into the restaurant parking lot and stopped near the front-door entrance. Exiting our car, we overheard someone say, "What's up with all these damn butterflies?" No more had he gotten this comment out of his mouth when Steph and I stopped in our tracks. The bushes on either side of the restaurant entrance were loaded with butterflies. Looking at each other, both Steph and I just knew, without a doubt, that these butterflies were Trista's sign to her daddy that she was okay. This was the sign he had asked for before she died. After sharing this revelation with the others, we took a short break and once again hit the highway heading north.

CHAPTER 51

§

STANDING BY THE GRAVESITE LISTENING to Fr. Delma offering words of peace, encouragement and closure was the format for our final good-bye. This place, however, although beautifully landscaped, wasn't comforting to me in the least.

I thought about how easy it would be to find Trista's grave in the future because erroneously mom and dad's tombstone with their birthdays engraved on it had already been placed where they would be laid to rest one day.

Dad had been quite proud for having prepared and completed all necessary arrangements for his and mom's burial one day, complete with purchase of the tombstone. On one sunny Sunday afternoon he brought us to the cemetery to show us where their plots were. He was not prepared to see that the tombstone was already there complete with engraving. It only needed one thing, his and mom's dates of death. Although, unnerved by the experience and even a little angry with the monument company about this major mix-up, he decided to leave the stone.

Trista died on August 4, 1984—only 25 days before her four-teenth birthday. To my knowledge, nothing significant was going on in the United States or the world at this time, but our world was forever changed. How does that work when a person is there with you for almost 14 years and then is suddenly not? How does anyone switch gears that quickly—to go from a family of four to a family of three?

When we stopped at a restaurant on the drive back to Kentucky, the hostess asked me, "How many are there in your party, please?" "Four," I said, to which our son quickly whispered to me, "Three, Mom." Saying it aloud made my stomach churn and I wasn't sure I could eat. At this moment I did know that our family had no choice but to begin a new journey although we were down one person.

§

CHAPTER 52

WHEN WE ARRIVED HOME, I hoped that rest would come. I knew our bodies and minds were so tired. However, it didn't come. How much rest does an 12-year-old boy really need? As soon as we stepped inside the front door, Stephan asked if he could go to play with his friends down the street. I settled into this new beginning by changing clothes and walking into Trista's room to just sit on her empty bed. Nothing had been changed or moved since the moment they took her away. I wouldn't allow it and had closed her bedroom door to ensure nothing was touched.

Thinking about all that had happened, I began needing evidence that she had been here. I picked up her pillow and the clothes she last wore to see if I could extract a scent of her. I could. Closing my eyes and holding her pillow to my face, I finally let the tears flow, crying and yelling into the pillow. I wailed in grief until there were no more tears. Exhausted, I put Trista's pillow back where it had been, left her room and closed the door. I decided that we would reserve this place for grief, for experiencing her presence, for private, disparaging moments. It was so intimate, so personal, a piece of her was still there.

CHAPTER 53

§

TRISTA WAS BURIED ON A Monday and by the following Tuesday, our family needed to jump back into life. Although, feeling crippled, disabled we needed to go back to work, to school and re-enter society. Isn't this the same recommendation doctors have for patients immediately following heart surgery or a hip replacement? They instruct their patients to get up as soon as possible after surgery because it may be detrimental to be down for too long. It assists the recovery process, they say. Does this rapid-recovery approach also apply to a family down a member? Who decided this was best and best for whom?

Since Steph worked nights, me days at the salon and Steph's 1984 school year hadn't yet begun, we discussed our plan. It turned out that I was the first to head back to work. I knew that my clients would be kind and the salon team had done an amazing job keeping the business on track. Still, I wasn't prepared for stepping back into the work I had truly loved before Trista got sick.

I would compare the "small talk" that first day to tearing my insides. It must have been tough for these people to know what to say to me. I'm sure that the things everyone said were nice, cordial courtesies—the updates about their kids attending which universities, grandma who was back in the hospital and the pastor whose congregation was fed up with him. I heard it all but never became engaged in any of it. It did distract me from the terrible pain in my chest, though.

By God's grace alone, the day was about over. Some nice hairdos had been achieved by all and I was grateful I had survived. Then I heard a client laughing, really belly-laughing, in response to a joke someone had shared. For some reason, her laughter made me so angry and I'm sure I gave the woman a "stink eye" look. She abruptly stopped laughing and quickly shut down her frivolity. She and I locked eyes; she whispered something to her stylist and stared back at me. The incident could not have been more uncomfortable for everyone present.

The only thing that I could figure out as far as why it made me so angry was that these people were all going about their day as usual, laughing, getting their hair done, exchanging stories like nothing had happened. How dare they be happy! Didn't they realize the tragic death of my daughter who was too young to die had just occurred last week? *What is wrong with these people?* I thought.

I realized that my anger could be a reoccurring problem. Maybe it was wrong for me to feel this way. I decided that, going forward, I would focus only on the client who was seated in my chair and no one else. Remaining attentive to one person at a time seemed less painful and gave me the ability to be nonjudgmental of everyone. They did not have a problem but clearly I did.

Thinking back about this incident and the woman who I believed inappropriately laughed, I know that she kept coming to our salon. Clearly, I had been rude and yet she was kind to keep coming back.

CHAPTER 54

§

FOR WEEKS OUR SMALL FAMILY went through the motions of life rather than authentically living the moments. It became obvious to me that our son, Stephan, was desperately trying to have a way to express his grief. Sometimes he and I would cry together and just hold each other. His dad used work as a means to buffer the pain of *his* loss. Keeping very busy seemed to help him. He didn't have as much time to think about everything—to dwell on missing Trista.

I recognized that it was important that we get expert support to be able to make some sense of the grief. So we scheduled weekly sessions for young Stephan and me to get grief counseling. However, Steph was not interested in this kind of help saying he did not need to pay someone to stir up his pain even more. I have decided that this is the most difficult aspect of grieving for a family. Each person needs to have the freedom to get through it in his or her own way. Grief is so personal, so intimate, and it is difficult to let someone share it with you. Maybe this is even more often true for an adult male.

As painful as Trista's loss was for me and young Stephan, it was important for the two of us to remember that Trista was Daddy's little girl. Steph adored Trista from the day she was born. In fact, their baby pictures looked so much alike that we would sometimes get them confused as far as which one was her dad's or Trista's. Flooding my thoughts were the many times that as a baby she laid on a blanket on our living room floor. Steph would lie next to her and talk to her making silly noises just to see her smile. They had bonded in a very special way.

In hindsight, I think that in my selfishness, I was just trying to survive each day. Aside from counseling sessions with Stephan, I did not discuss this terrible grief with anyone. I don't even remember discussing with Steph how much I missed Trista. I don't recall asking him how he was doing. Nor do I remember sitting down with Steph to create a plan about how we would go on from here. I know that statistically speaking, many couples who have lost children, get a divorce. The experience is just so painful that all communication shuts down. Everyone wants someone or something to blame. And sometimes one parent may assume responsibility for the death.

Although I was determined not to fall into this widespread broken-marriage statistic, I could not say that there was any special effort on my part to keep this from happening. I believe that only by God's grace were we spared this additional loss in our home. It is as though He lifted us up and enabled us to keep outside the realm of arguing and accusatory judgments. Nevertheless, all thoughts of marital intimacy had vanished.

CHAPTER 55

§

THE WEEKS TURNED INTO MONTHS. It seemed like it was now the right time to give away some of Trista's clothes—maybe to someone at church who could use them. I carefully selected which outfits to part with. I gave Trista's clothes to a family from our parish one day after Mass. It made me smile to watch how elated the little girl was with the bag of clothes. I envisioned that it made Trista smile too. It was a first step.

Life seemed to be moving at a reasonable pace again. We continued to go through the typical motions of our former life when Trista was with us, but it was not normal. However, what is normal? I was blessed with the gift of being able to act okay even if I was not. This skill was acquired by being fourth in the sibling food chain. Outwardly, things looked fine, but inside I was dying. In fact, I did want to die, to be released from pain that never let up for one minute while awake or even during the night. It did not matter where I was or what I was doing. It did not matter that the three of us were truly blessed to have each other and we were working successfully getting back on our feet financially. Nothing really mattered. Trista was gone and I could not bear it.

We were successfully completing all necessary actions to keep going and yet no single day ever stood out to me at this time. Life was a blob of time to get through until I could go home and sleep. That was the only space where I rested in peace. Have you ever been driving your car while so deep in thought that you could not remember how you made it to your street? If so, you can relate to a particular night for my going home from work. That was one of those occasions for me.

I am not one who speeds, but my mind certainly was not in an alert state of consciousness for safe driving. I turned onto Winding Creek Trail as I had done many times before and I was so deep in thought that I drove right past our house. I kept going down our road when I suddenly heard a thump like I had hit something with one of the tires. Thinking it was probably a toy or ball a child had left in the street, I stopped the car and got out to investigate. When I saw the little smashed puppy under my tire, I became hysterical. I screamed and cried realizing what I had thoughtlessly done. Knowing I had to go to talk to the neighbor whose house was nearest me, I walked up onto their porch to tell whoever was home what I had done.

I knocked as hard as I could as I continued to cry uncontrollably. A woman came to the door who I didn't know well and had only occasionally seen outside in her yard. After explaining what I had done and that it was entirely my fault, I asked for forgiveness and told her I would buy her family a new puppy although I knew that would not bring this one back.

Heaving deep breaths because I had been crying so hard, I waited to hear the woman's response. I deserved for her to be angry with me; in fact I wanted her to yell at me. She just stood there and looked at me with tears in her eyes. She opened the door and pulled me to herself to hug me saying, "I know who you are and what your family has been through. This is a puppy and we can get another one. I will get my husband to get the puppy out of the street. You go home to your family and know that it is all right. We will be fine, Shirley. Go home." So I did, still crying—for me, for us, for the family whose puppy I had killed, for any other reason I could find. I cried until I had no more tears that day.

Each morning I arrived early at the salon and sat in the parking lot for a while to collect myself before walking through the door to see people. I was so broken that I would hit the steering wheel as hard as I could while pleading with God to give me some peace. I would plead with Him to take the pain away. I begged Him to send healing because I did not believe I could handle the grief one more day. Then I would get out of my car and walk into the salon. I would wear my artificial smile ready to greet the beautiful unsuspecting clients and staff who were expecting courtesy and kindness. They deserved that from me.

Always grateful for one more successful day under my belt with my stealth, grief-stricken personality intact, I would then drive home and go straight to the bathroom to get cleaned up before fixing dinner. Getting the hairspray off in a soaking bath was usually therapeutic because it allowed me time to mentally leave the business behind and emotionally prepare to spend quality time with my family. Once Trista was gone, the therapy time turned into a desperate escape when I would scream into a damp washcloth stuffed in my mouth while beating the sides of the bathtub until my fists were raw and bruised.

Thirty minutes or so of this activity somehow gave me strength to complete the required activities of the day to be with my family. I had grave concerns that I might be headed for a mental breakdown. Not knowing how that really felt since I had no prior experience, I determined that *if* I were headed for a breakdown, I probably would not know it. This line of thinking gave me some peace. I felt that beating on the steering wheel or the tub to cope with a day was safe survival techniques. In retrospect, my *big* mistake was keeping my techniques to myself. In hindsight, I wish I could have been as open with my husband and my son as Trista forced me to be when she and I were at Vanderbilt. It was liberating that she and I could cry together.

I believed that for me to be a strong Christian woman of faith, I should not need to break down like this so frequently. I truly knew where Trista was; I did not lose her. I just was not sure where *I* was and so the pretenses continued until one day I simply could not do it anymore.

Many weeks after Trista's death, I went to work at the salon and my staff asked if we could have a short staff meeting. Agreeing to this, before the salon opened for business we all huddled near the center of the salon. One woman on our salon team nervously cleared her throat and said, "Shirley, we know that what you've been through must have been really tough but we're a little disappointed that you never laugh in here anymore. Even customers are talking about it to us. It seems like every time your church doors are open, you rush to go to a service. You need to give this business more of your attention and we just wanted to say that to you."

All the eyes of the salon team were on me waiting for a response. If one of them had stabbed me in the stomach and twisted the knife, I could not have hurt more than I did now from their words. Stunned and shocked, I just stood there. I'm sure that anger showed on my face but I knew it was important to remain silent. I asked God to help me and praise God He did. I said the following: "I appreciate how difficult this must be to tell me these things and I do believe you all mean well. But, I promise you that it is taking every ounce of courage and strength I can muster just to get through each day. This salon is where I need to be. Yet, given the choice, I'd rather be at home or at church. The only place I find peace is at church and I will continue to go there at every opportunity." I did not want them to see me cry at this time, so I left the salon and went straight to our priest's rectory. The pretense was over and I had not been as emotionally stealthy as I thought I had been after all.

Greeting me with his usual friendly and calm demeanor, Fr. Delma invited me in. Immediately cutting to the chase, I let him know that my pain was too great without Trista and I did not want to live anymore without her. Then the floodgates of tears gushed forth as never before. I cried and cried, and then looked up to see Fr. Delma crying with me. Big tears were flowing down his cheeks as rapidly as they were running down mine. Both of us cried until there were no more tears left. We wiped our faces and he began talking to me about making a deal with him. Incredibly exhausted from all the crying, I listened intently. "So you want to die, too. Well, here's my deal. You ask God to take your life, if that's what you really want.

If He doesn't take it, you wait it out until He's ready for you to go. We both know that taking your life is not an option. It's not yours to take. But, if He takes it, that's okay. Do we have a deal?" I agreed, and then left the rectory for the short drive home.

Once home I thought about my time with Fr. Delma and I was grateful for him and how he truly ministered to me. If he had laid a ton of scripture on me, given me theological doctrine about suicide or even asked me to pray with him, I believe I would have been totally turned off. The best gift Fr. Delma gave me that day was to simply sit and cry with me. I desperately needed someone who loved Trista to cry with me. He offered me an honest deal. So, I prayed for God to take me. At each new day I grew more certain that one day I would not need to pray this prayer anymore.

Fr. Delma sought me out the following Sunday after Mass and asked how I was doing. He said that he had a plan for me. He explained that he believed it was time for me to get my mind off of *me*, and onto other people. Father wanted me to learn how to be a Eucharistic Minister and on Sunday afternoons to take Holy Communion to Catholics who were patients in our local hospital. Rather than being offended by his assessment of my condition, I knew he truly wanted what was best for me. I was happy that he spoke the truth in love when I most needed to hear it. After discussing this potential service opportunity with Steph, I agreed.

One thing our priest clearly explained was that ministering to hospitalized Catholics involved more of a commitment than merely serving them Communion. It was my job to also visit with each person for a little while, if the person indicated that he or she wanted me to do so.

Trained and armed with all necessary and sacred items, I was eager to serve in this way. Steph even went with me the first few times. As I made the rounds, I thought of Trista and remembered how she and I visited the moms at Vanderbilt and I would cut and style their hair. Trista talked to their children. She was on the same spiritual plane as Fr. Delma. Why didn't I think about serving instead of wallowing in my own selfishness?!

Some of the people we visited were lonely and so appreciated the company while others preferred to receive Communion only. Following the lead of the patient, we completed visitation of every person on the list and I knew that something inside me had begun to change. Steph and I later recounted the experiences that we had with each patient and recognized that everything seemed better—almost bearable that day.

I continued to serve as a Eucharistic Minister at the hospital and began to look forward to this time each Sunday. Knowing some people were suffering and I was bringing them Jesus gave purpose and meaning to my life in addition to my being a wife, mom and friend. I found that I did not need to hit the steering wheel *or* the sides of the tub to get through a day. Nevertheless the crying binges still had a life of their own. I could not seem to control them. I knew that it must have been upsetting to others and made them feel uncomfortable around me.

One Sunday after Mass and after I received the Eucharist that I planned to take to the hospital, the little girl that I had given Trista's clothes to, ran up to me. She could hardly wait to show me how beautiful she looked in Trista's dress. It fit her perfectly and she *did* look beautiful. However, what she shared with me took my breath away. She said, "Miss Shirley, last night I saw Trista. I know she was blind, couldn't walk and lost all of her hair but in my dream she didn't look like that at all. Trista was wearing a dress, was bare-footed, had all her hair and was dancing! I asked her, 'Trista, how can you be dancing?' and she just kept on looking at me and smiling and dancing. She's so happy."

O, the way that this child so vividly described Trista to me. I knew that Trista had come to her and I hugged this little girl so tightly for a long time until she wiggled loose. Thanking God repeatedly in my mind, a peace came that I am unable to describe or explain to this day.

Charged up and exuberant after hearing about this child's dream, I headed for the hospital once again. After I had seen all the Catholic patients except one, I stopped in on a new patient. It was a man who was about 45 or 50 years old. He asked me if I could stay a little while after he received Holy Communion. What he shared with me was like a story out of a novel. After asking for prayer, he wanted me to hear about what just happened that landed him in the hospital.

He explained that he began losing the use of his legs—something like nerve damage—that then progressed to weaken his arms, too. When he could no longer stand, his wife and two teenage daughters brought him to the hospital. After many tests and a continuing physical decline, the doctor decided to test a strand of his hair and a fingernail to check for toxins. They found toxins all right; it was arsenic. It seems that his wife had been slowly poisoning him. During the investigation the police uncovered that his wife intended to kill him, get the life insurance money and run off with another man that she had been seeing for a long time.

The life this man thought he had no longer existed for him and he was in deep despair. Not knowing if a full recovery was even possible for him, he wept as he finished the story by telling me that his wife had just been arrested. "I loved her," he said, "and had no idea that she hated me so much. I had no idea."

After listening in shock without saying a word, I asked the man if I could pray with him before I left. I thanked God for this man's life being spared and for the wisdom of the doctors to find the cause of his illness. Then, I asked God to hold this man up in grace as he got through these challenging times. He thanked me and I left, crying for him this time, instead of myself.

After I confirmed the accuracy of the details in this man's story, I asked God to forgive me for being so selfish in my grief. I had lost a daughter to illness while this man had his entire world turned upside down in a most horrific way. Fr. Delma knew exactly what he was doing by sending me to the hospital. In serving others, my pain was lessened—my mind was off of me. It is interesting how that works—interesting how God works.

CHAPTER 56

§

SERVING COMMUNION AT THE HOSPITAL was helpful and it temporarily got my mind off me as well as off of the overwhelming grief. However, it still seemed that dealing with all the feelings and emotions in a constructive way was virtually impossible.

Even though I had not expressed this deep need out loud, a good friend brought me a book that she believed would be helpful. It must have been apparent, even though I tried to disguise it, that I was really struggling. I could not seem to find our "new normal"—a lifestyle or approach to life without Trista.

On Death and Dying, by Elizabeth Kubler-Ross, was the book she gave me. After reading it cover-to-cover, it was evident to me that there are stages in which one grieves. This woman had dedicated her life to learning about dying and grief, a subject we usually recoil from—even with our dearest friends. Since this is not a desirable topic, even though it will affect us all eventually, we often don't learn about this important part of our lives until it just happens.

It became obvious to me that the stages of grief I was experiencing were "textbook." However, I felt that there was something wrong about my grieving process that I couldn't identify. Whatever it was, was so wrong that I began having terrible nightmares that were beginning to suck the life right out of me. Now grieving as well as sleep-deprived, I found myself even less equipped to heal or to help my family move toward healing.

During this time in my life a dear friend from church, Margaret Coy, asked me if I would be interested in going to a church service with her in Owensboro, Kentucky. To provide you a little background about my friend Margaret: she was disabled from the effects of polio. I remembered hearing about polio when I was a child. My mom used to warn us kids not to play in ditches filled with water or in any standing puddles because we might get polio.

Margaret shared with me that when she was married years ago, she had three children and lived in a housing complex where many other children also lived. One day she noticed a small child, who was obviously a renegade from his mom's watchful eye. He was playing in the parking area. Envisioning this to be a potentially dangerous situation, Margaret scooped up this small child and took him home. What no one knew at that time was that this child had polio and Margaret contracted it from this child.

As Margaret physically struggled with polio, she was at a disadvantage maintaining a household plus caring for her three children. She eventually needed a wheelchair. As it became increasingly difficult for her to care for her family, Margaret's husband left her. Trusting that God would help in all her needs, she and her three children moved into low-income housing where Margaret raised her children from her wheelchair—not an easy task.

Although Margaret seemed to adapt to this physical disability, she often had bouts with difficult breathing and needed to be on oxygen for extended periods of time.

Margaret was my confidante. For some strange reason I felt comfortable telling her the most silly and intimate things. I knew that she would never judge me. An example is that one Sunday as we were walking out of church and I was pushing Margaret's wheelchair, Steph said something—I can't remember what—that embarrassed me to the bone. Margaret, reading the expression of horror on my face, pulled me to herself so my ear was near her lips and commented, "You didn't say it and there's no reason for you to be upset or embarrassed by that." She was, of course, right and my embarrassment and negative emotions were quickly put in check.

The day came for the Owensboro church service that I had agreed to attend with Margaret. On the way there, Margaret explained that this was a healing service that would be led by Fr. Glahn. Wow! I was thrilled and looking forward to this now. I held Fr. Glahn in such high regard and I wondered if we would actually witness God's healing. Since Margaret was one of the most committed prayer warriors I had ever met, I believed we were both in for a huge blessing. Margaret believed that every person could contribute something, no matter the disability, and she was the one that had organized our church's prayer chain.

We got to the service and I took my seat in a pew while Margaret's wheelchair was now locked down and positioned at the end of the pew. At the front of the church near the altar, Fr. Glahn was standing and proceeded to explain what to expect at this service. He reminded us that God does whatever He chooses. Some healing can be immediate whereas it could be a healing over time. He talked about different kinds of healing, some of which I had previously heard little about and some I knew nothing about at all. Besides physical healing, categories of healing included healing of memories and healing through forgiveness.

Fr. Glahn took us through a healing of memories—from conception to the present, as a group. Then he introduced us to a missionary nun who would be assisting him with the next portion of the service. The healing service now became personal. We were invited to come forward individually and form a line for either Fr. Glahn or the nun. They pray over each of us by laying their hands on us in a way that would address whatever healing intention we petitioned from God. I was psyched up about this part and I leaned over to Margaret asking if she was ready for me to wheel her up front to receive her healing. At this, Margaret gave me the funniest look, and said, "I didn't come here for me to be healed. I came here for you to receive healing.

You're a mess." I was embarrassed that I had presumed why we were there—not to mention a little hurt by her words. However, I knew she knew I desperately needed help. "Go on up there and get in Fr. Glahn's line. Ask for peace. That's what you need, right?" she said.

It was uncomfortable thinking about going up there and getting in line to ask for help—to ask for healing. I inched my way to the center of the aisle and joined the line for healing through prayers of Fr. Glahn. I was like a shy schoolgirl checking back to be sure her mom is still watching her as I kept looking back at Margaret. She just smiled and gave me a wave of her hand directing me to keep moving forward.

This was the only time in my life that I could remember being grateful that the line was long. I hoped that by the time that it was my turn, I'd have the courage to ask God for the peace I desperately wanted. Margaret was right about me. It took a lot of courage for her to love me enough to get me there.

Listening to the beautiful background music and knowing Fr. Glahn as my friend, I knew it would be okay. That's how I felt until about the fifth person ahead of me. A man fell to the ground with an expression on his face like he was in some sort of a euphoric trance. The next person in line did the same. I immediately thought, it's time for me to shift over to the nun's line and I quickly did.

There were only three people ahead of me in the nun's line. I was feeling much better about asking for peace. People continued falling to the ground in Fr. Glahn's line and male attendants were now on guard to ensure that those falling would not hit their heads. They were dropping like flies over there. I was so glad to be in the nun's line!

My turn came and as I stood in front of the little nun I wondered what words she would use to pray over me for peace. Her eyes were kind and I immediately noticed that her fingernails were stained almost black. Not knowing what sort of missionary work she supported, I surmised from her hands that it was somewhat earthy in nature—in the real trenches somewhere.

Very softly, she asked, "What healing do you want to receive from God?" "For peace," I responded just as softly. Then she laid her small hands over the top of my head, closed her eyes and began praying so quietly that I could not hear what she was saying. That was the last thing I remember before hitting the ground. I truly did not know what was happening but I *did* know that I didn't want it to be over. I did not want to get up. I had been given a taste of what I had asked for—pure peace. It had been a long time since I felt at peace.

When I did stand up again, I went directly back to the pew near Margaret. She was smiling from ear to ear. "What happened?" I asked. "You were slain in the Spirit, "she answered. Not having any idea what that meant, I thanked God for it and trusted that it was a good thing. For that short time, I did have perfect peace. I prayed for that feeling again but I could not seem to get it back.

CHAPTER 57

§

THE NIGHTMARES CONTINUED AND THE lack of sleep kept dragging me down. It was at this time that Tara told me about a class,
taught by our local Episcopalian church's pastor. The class was about
dream interpretations. *Come on*, I thought. *Who does that, let alone a
pastor?* This seemed a little out there to me, but both Steph and I
knew Pastor Bob because we had served on Christian retreat teams
together. I decided that I had absolutely nothing to lose if I went.

The setting in my nightmares was at the top of the hill on the
Christ the King property very near the church. I needed a ride home
from church and would tell potential drivers that our house is close
and that it wouldn't take long if they would please give me a ride.
In the dream, a driver pulls up to where I am standing and offers to
take me home. I believe that since this person has just come from
our church service as I did, that it would be all right even if I didn't
know this man. I get into the car and before I could even get my
seatbelt fastened, he speeds down the grassy hill, instead of taking
the access road to the main road.

In a panic I look at this driver and yell, "What are you doing? Let
me out!" As he turns his head toward mine, his face becomes devilish
looking and he responds, "I'll never let you out!" Then, as always, at
this point in the dream, I wake up.

At the first dream interpretation class with Pastor Bob, he taught
us about interpretations typical to Western culture. I had not considered dreams had cultural bias but it made sense. Father told us

that in our culture that if you dream about a house, the house is you. If you dream that you are driving a car, you are feeling in control. If someone else is driving the car in your dream and you are the passenger, you are feeling out of control. Once the first session had ended, I knew that I needed to learn more and asked to schedule a counseling session with Pastor Bob.

Several days later I met with Pastor Bob in his office. I described the recurring nightmare. He was quiet for what seemed like a long time. Then he asked if he could pray with me about my problem. After the prayer he said, "Why do you think you are stronger than anyone else? Why are you trying not to grieve or to cry when you are in great pain? That is not the devil in the car with you. That is grief. It's a lie that grief will never let go of you. It will and it does." Taking in his every word, I burst into tears. I thought that since I am a Christian, I should be dealing with the loss of Trista in a way that was a witness to others. Pastor Bob explained to me that being "real" is the best witness there is. He said that no one can be constantly inconsistent with who they are or what they are feeling. It was liberating. That day I decided to cry if I felt like it, wherever and whenever I felt like it. That would be real.

It was such freedom to be myself with my family, friends and at work. I simply could not get caught up in how everyone else responded to my crying anymore. It also gave Steph and Stephan freedom to cry, get angry and grieve in their unique ways. Praise God for this gift! I did hope that one day I would have control enough to cry at my convenience and in privacy. However, I would need to wait for this. Who would have guessed that God would provide exactly what I needed at this time through a dream interpretation class offered by an Episcopalian priest? God was continuing to open my eyes with His providing nature. It seemed to come from the most unusual places and from people I would never have looked to for help.

CHAPTER 58

§

BEFORE WE KNEW IT, ADVENT arrived—the preparation time prior to Christmas. Since we seemed to be spending more time than usual at our church attending additional weekday Masses and special services, I was looking forward to celebrating Jesus' birthday and to decorating our home, inside and out.

With gifts wrapped and food prepared, Steph, Stephan and I went to midnight Mass. It was beautiful. As was tradition for our family, we planned to go to bed after late Mass then wake up early on Christmas morning to open presents and eat a giant feast.

As I went to bed on Christmas Eve, I remembered a Christmas long ago when the four of us were living in our first home in Akron on Wise Street. The children were young—Trista four and Stephan three. We had just tucked the children into bed and Steph and I put the gifts from Santa under the tree in anticipation of a perfect Christmas morning.

I remember hearing noises coming from downstairs that long ago Christmas. I awoke and looked at the clock on the nightstand. It beamed three A.M. I quietly crept down the stairs to see what was causing the noises. Shocked, I saw that Trista and Stephan had just finished opening all of their presents and were having a great time playing with them. At first I was angry because they had jumped the gun and we didn't get the pleasure of watching them open their gifts. I was able to let my personal disappointment go and went down to join the fun. It was not long before they couldn't keep their eyes open, no matter how excited they were. I was able to coax them back to bed. All four of us slept in that Christmas.

Finally, drifting off to sleep with that special Christmas memory still on my mind, I actually rested well until I heard Stephan get up. After peeking out of the bedroom door, I whispered to Steph that we should get up, too.

Grabbing coffee and orange juice we three settled into our usual seats in the living room in preparation for opening our gifts. I began to visually scan the room to notice, that according to our family traditions, all was in order. Except Trista wasn't there. I instantly became physically sick to my stomach and could not stop crying. Poor Steph and Stephan had no way to console me and it was a horrible scene that wasn't anything like any of us had hoped for this first Christmas without her. I finally told them, "I just can't do this without Trista." I went to our bedroom, shut the door and lay on the bed and cried myself to sleep.

What happened next was miraculous. It was so real to me because I could actually see myself on our bed. Trista was standing beside me watching me cry. "What's wrong, Mom?" she asked. "I just can't do Christmas without you," I said. Trista took a moment and responded, "You know, Mom, how it is when you spend the night at someone else's house and sleep in someone else's bed, that it isn't ever as good a sleep as when you're in your own bed, in your own home? I'm home now, Mom." Then Trista put her hand on my arm and smiled. She looked so healthy, and happy.

I woke up remembering every detail of this dream and shared it with Steph and Stephan. We all cried, opened our presents making it through our first Christmas without her. But, in truth, it was then that I realized that Trista had been with us all along. How else could she have known that her mom was in such despair? Trista gave me the best present of all—knowing she was "home."

CHAPTER 59

§

IF SOMEONE HAD TOLD US that Trista and I would spend over a year at Vanderbilt Hospital *or* that so many people, many of whom we never met, would come to our aid to provide for our family's needs during this 18-month trial, I'm sure that we would not have believed them. As we live through a trial, gratefully, we have no idea that it is a trial. Nor, thankfully, do we know how long a *really* hard situation will last or that it may never be over in this lifetime. God is so good to give us only one moment at a time. Otherwise, we would be unable to stand the pain or the fear of some of these trials.

Several years passed and our family continued to jump into life with work, school and church as we had once done. However, we were never the same as before we lost Trista. We took trips and visited friends. But we were now different. It is as though we now lived with a secret that made us different from anyone else. We now knew that life is fleeting and that things do not always turn out as we plan.

When clients shared with me at the salon that one of their family members had surgery to remove a cancer and that the doctors assured the family that all the cancer was now gone, I could never believe it. Although, I don't believe that I had become completely cynical, I do believe I now understood that no one could possibly know if surgeons or treatment eradicates a disease. We would be naïve to think so. I began to believe that we are all in the same position before God whether we are sick with cancer or seemingly well. Our lives are totally in His hands to do with as He pleases. That said, He is a loving God and sees life's events far differently than we view them. Scripture says that His ways are not our ways and I believe that is true. I choose now to be at no one's mercy but God's.

Life is not perfect and I now knew that for a fact. I would listen to friends and family members share their plans about where their kids would go to college or where the family would go on a long-planned-for-vacation. I would think to myself, *maybe these plans will unfold as envisioned and maybe they won't.*

Also, I know that I rarely felt *real* joy. It still didn't seem right to feel happy. I did resolve to be happy for others. That seemed good enough for me then. Nevertheless, I did hope that one day I could know joy again.

CHAPTER 60

§

I̲T̲ ̲B̲E̲C̲A̲M̲E̲ ̲I̲N̲C̲R̲E̲A̲S̲I̲N̲G̲L̲Y̲ ̲D̲I̲F̲F̲I̲C̲U̲L̲T̲ ̲T̲O̲ live in our Winding Creek Trail home due to all the memories of Trista, as well as, her dying in her bedroom. We decided to sell our house and build a new one in Hanson, Kentucky.

My dad called our new home "The Mansion on the Hill." I'm not sure that I would call it a mansion but it was most certainly situated at the top of a steep hill. We used architectural plans taken from the replica of a Virginia townhouse in the late 1700s, and we knew we would love living there. This home would symbolize a new beginning for our family and young Stephan believed it had potential to be a real "babe magnet."

Building this new home occupied our time every single day and it seemed like a constructive use of time—a healthy preoccupation. Because our Winding Creek Trail home sold quickly, we moved into a small rental home while our new home was being built. Each day we would go to the construction site to inspect the day of work. Also, we would just walk around the yard dreaming out loud about how our new life there would be filled with new traditions and memories.

We were in our home only a short time and it already seemed perfect for the three of us. I began to look forward to waking up in our new bedroom and going to work. I knew life could never go back to the way it was when Trista was with us. I began to pray for wisdom, discernment and guidance for our future. Certainly, these were good things to pray for and I was sure that God would answer these prayers.

I tried to be more outwardly jovial at this time but just could not. My "silly factor" that I once enjoyed seemed to have died with Trista and I didn't want it back without her.

One day at the salon I was styling one of my customer's hair when she began telling me a joke. This joke was rather long and involved and I struggled to follow her story. When the punch line finally surfaced, I abruptly laughed out loud because it really was the funniest joke I had ever heard. I laughed so hard that tears came to my eyes and everyone around me took notice. The salon was packed with customers. Suddenly, realizing I was laughing loudly, I stopped. It hit me that I had no right to laugh with Trista gone. I recognized at that moment that I was restricting myself from being too happy. I realized then that it really was okay to laugh. I laughed even more and it felt so good, so real and so right. That joke, that laugh, was the turning point toward healing, toward becoming this real person who loved life, loved people, God and Trista.

That night when I soaked in the tub, instead of beating the sides, I folded my hands in prayer to thank God for this precious customer, her funny joke and for a real laugh. Praise God! I could laugh again and it was okay.

CHAPTER 61

§

Trista died in 1984. By 1988, our family life demonstrated that we were on a path to wholeness—a new path and a more mature faith. At this time we decided to sell our salon business. The adventurous dream of having our own salon had waned greatly. It was like I no longer needed it and preferred to simply do only what I loved doing—dressing hair.

After going to work at another salon, The Hair Doc, I was approached and asked to fill a training position for a hair company. It would afford me some travel time. And with Stephan now in his final years of high school, it seemed like a good time to venture out a little. Steph agreed.

We continued to be involved in our faith community at Christ the King Church and participated in our Share Groups.

One day, while praying at home, I had the ridiculous idea that we had just built this beautiful new home for someone else. I shared this thought with my husband. Both of us discounted the idea. I went to work at The Hair Doc that day and a client gave me the inside scoop that the Goodyear plant where Steph worked would soon be shutting down. In denial and disbelief, I went home to discuss with Steph some potential options for our future. Steph was not convinced I had received totally accurate information.

However, it *was* accurate information. And before I could get my arms around this sudden change of plans, Steph was relocated to Marysville, Ohio. He would live there with his brother Greg in a hotel room until my sister Pam and I could get our homes sold.

Thankfully our homes sold fairly quickly and we four were once again in new locations ready to begin new lives. This transition was difficult for us and I am still not sure why. Maybe it was because we missed our dear son who was now in the Navy and he would never know this new place as his home. Maybe it was because we were leaving our faith community where many people knew us and had known about Trista. Maybe it was difficult for all of these reasons. But we certainly found this move difficult.

Pam and Greg found a new home rather quickly. Steph and I lived in an apartment for a while to recalibrate our future plans, become familiar with the area and to find a new church home. After visiting several churches, we found Our Lady of Lourdes Church in Marysville. We felt that we could help support a faith community there. Everyone made us feel welcome.

On our very first visit after Mass at Our Lady of Lourdes Church, we introduced ourselves to the organist who invited us to sing in the choir the next Sunday. "But we don't know any of the songs," I said. "No problem! You can learn as you go. Jump in. I'll be looking for you next week," she said. That was that, and we did as she recommended. It was best to just jump in.

Soon after finding a church, we found a home in Dublin, Ohio. However, we eventually moved to Plain City where we lived in the country nearer the Goodyear plant where Steph worked, and nearer to our new church. It was perfect!

When meeting all these new people at our church and in the community, new acquaintances would always ask about our family and also, eventually ask, "And do you have any children?" To which I always answered, "Yes, we have a son who is in the military, Stephan II and a daughter, Trista, who is in heaven. She was almost 14 and died from brain cancer." It seemed easier if I just went ahead and explained why she died.

It always seemed right to us to mention that we have a daughter although she was not with us physically. Ninety-nine percent of the time when we told people, whom we had just met, about Trista, they would kindly say, "I'm so sorry. That must have been horrible. I could never get through that." I never knew exactly what to say next, so I would generally smile and begin to inquire about their families.

Not long after moving into our current home in Plain City, Ohio, I was on a business trip to conduct training in New York City for the hair company I now worked for full time. Arriving at LaGuardia, I got a cab to take me into Manhattan. It was about a 20-minute drive, so I sat back in my seat to just relax and check out the scenery. The cab driver broke the silence by asking me where I'd come from, followed by questions about my family. I gave my usual responses about Steph and Stephan and concluded by telling him about Trista. Instead of the usual responses, I had always gotten after sharing about her illness and death, he said to me, "And what did you learn from that?"

What a profound question, I thought, as I pondered an honest response. My mind began spinning with all the possible answers that I might give him. Then it occurred to me, *what kind of cab driver asks such a question?* By this time, I had been to New York City many times. Never once had a New York City cab driver ever engaged me in any sort of meaningful conversation, let alone rocked me to the core by asking such a question as this. I laughed out loud and said to the cab driver, "God is incredible. He sent everything we needed, exactly when we needed it and how we needed it. In fact, He continues to do that every single day. Think about it. I'm in this cab with you, and you just asked me the perfect question."

Made in the USA
Middletown, DE
15 October 2018